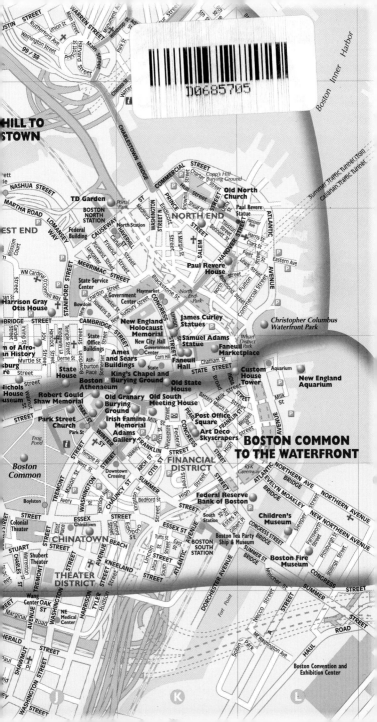

Boston's
25Best

by Sue Gordon

Fodor's Travel Publications
New York • Toronto • London • Sydney • Auckland
www.fodors.com

How to Use This Book

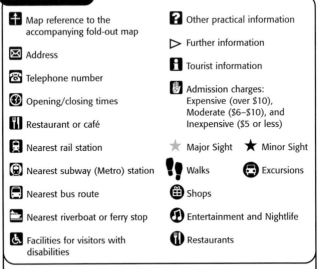

KEY TO SYMBOLS

🕂 Map reference to the accompanying fold-out map

✉ Address

☎ Telephone number

🕒 Opening/closing times

🍴 Restaurant or café

🚉 Nearest rail station

Ⓜ Nearest subway (Metro) station

🚌 Nearest bus route

⛴ Nearest riverboat or ferry stop

♿ Facilities for visitors with disabilities

❓ Other practical information

▷ Further information

ℹ Tourist information

✋ Admission charges: Expensive (over $10), Moderate ($6–$10), and Inexpensive ($5 or less)

★ Major Sight ★ Minor Sight

👣 Walks 🚐 Excursions

🛍 Shops

🎵 Entertainment and Nightlife

🍴 Restaurants

This guide is divided into four sections

• Essential Boston: An introduction to the city and tips on making the most of your stay.

• Boston by Area: We've broken the city into five areas, and recommended the best sights, shops, entertainment venues, nightlife and restaurants in each one. Suggested walks help you to explore on foot.

• Where to Stay: The best hotels, whether you're looking for luxury, budget or something in between.

• Need to Know: The info you need to make your trip run smoothly, including getting about by public transportation, weather tips, emergency phone numbers and useful websites.

Navigation In the Boston by Area chapter, we've given each area its own color, which is also used on the locator maps throughout the book and the map on the inside front cover.

Maps The fold-out map accompanying this book is a comprehensive street plan of Boston. The grid on this fold-out map is the same as the grid on the locator maps within the book. We've given grid references within the book for each sight and listing.

Contents

ESSENTIAL BOSTON	4–18
Introducing Boston	4–5
A Short Stay in Boston	6–7
Top 25	8–9
Shopping	10–11
Shopping by Theme	12
Boston by Night	13
Eating Out	14
Restaurants by Cuisine	15
If You Like…	16–18

BOSTON BY AREA	19–106
BEACON HILL TO CHARLESTOWN	**20–46**
Area Map	22–23
Sights	24–39
Walk	40
Shopping	41–42
Entertainment and Nightlife	43
Restaurants	45–46

BOSTON COMMON TO THE WATERFRONT	47–62
Area Map	48–49
Sights	50–56
Walk	57
Shopping	58
Entertainment and Nightlife	59–60
Restaurants	61–62

BACK BAY AND THE SOUTH END	63–84
Area Map	64–65
Sights	66–78
Walk	79
Shopping	80–81
Entertainment and Nightlife	82–83
Restaurants	84

CAMBRIDGE	85–98
Area Map	86–87
Sights	88–92
Walk	93
Shopping	94–95
Entertainment and Nightlife	96–97
Restaurants	97–98

FARTHER AFIELD	99–106
Area Map	100–101
Sights	102–104
Excursions	105–106

WHERE TO STAY	107–112
Introduction	108
Budget Hotels	109
Mid-Range Hotels	110–111
Luxury Hotels	112

NEED TO KNOW	113–125
Planning Ahead	114–115
Getting There	116–117
Getting Around	118–119
Essential Facts	120–123
Timeline	124–125

Introducing Boston

From its 17th-century beginnings as a British colony, Boston has been a town of undeniable independent spirit. Its plucky revolutionaries earned it that reputation early on, and the city itself has upheld the tradition ever since.

Massachusetts has led many of the country's most important movements: public education, the abolition of slavery, women's equality and gay rights. Boston and Cambridge, its sister city across the Charles River (in this book, references to Boston include Cambridge), have been at the forefront of these campaigns.

The city's dedication to culture and learning is well known, and can be seen in its world-class museums, concert halls and libraries, and in the countless college campuses. Even the music clubs, galleries and movie theaters have their own histories.

Meanwhile, Boston's quality of life is equally high out of doors. The string of parks and public spaces designed by Frederick Law Olmsted (collectively known as the "Emerald Necklace") runs through the city, providing stunning and well-maintained green space in many a neighborhood. Water is almost always nearby or visible, from the Charles River Esplanade of Back Bay to the downtown area bordering Boston Harbor. And Boston's architecture is some of the most beautiful in the country: as often as not, Victorian brownstones share blocks with art deco buildings and contemporary skyscrapers.

Of course, none of these perks comes cheap. Boston's real estate is some of the most expensive in the country, and is seemingly ever on the rise. That's largely because, unlike many American cities, it has made urban living desirable, so its residents are willing to spend what's necessary. All in all, there are few cities in America more worth taking up residence in—or visiting.

Facts + Figures

- **The "T" was the US's first subway system. The first section opened in 1897.**
- **Boston Common was the first public park in America.**
- **Harvard University was the first college in North America.**

ODD FACTS

- Some 58 percent of Boston is built on landfill.
- Boston Light, on Little Brewster Island, was the first lighthouse in the United States (1716). It is still in operation.
- The Boston University Bridge is the only place in the world where a boat can sail under a train driving under a car driving under a plane.

LOCAL PASSIONS

● Ice cream (they eat more of it in Boston than any other city in the US).
● Baseball (traffic brings the area around Fenway Park to a halt for every game).
● Music (from local bands to symphony orchestras).

GETTING YOUR BEARINGS

Boston Common and the Public Garden lie at the heart of Boston. To their north is the old residential area of Beacon Hill. Southeast of the Common are the Theater District and Chinatown. The Freedom Trail, which starts on the Common, runs northeast through Old Boston, past Faneuil Hall to the Italian North End. Across the Charles River lies Harvard Square in Cambridge.

A Short Stay in Boston

DAY 1

Morning Arrive at the parking lot of the **New England Aquarium** (▷ 53) at 8.30 and duck into the boulangerie at **Sel de la Terre** (▷ 62) for its selection of fresh-baked breads, croissants and coffee. When the Aquarium opens at 9, walk its corridors to see both exotic and local sealife.

Mid-morning Make your way to **Faneuil Hall and Marketplace** (▷ 26) perusing the artist carts and watching the street performers along the way. Then walk past City Hall on to Tremont Street, and take a right on Beacon Street for a walk over historic **Beacon Hill** (▷ 24–25). After admiring the gold-domed **State House** (▷ 35), pass behind it down Mount Vernon Street, and take in posh **Louisburg Square** (▷ 24–25) and quaint, cobbled Acorn Street.

Lunch At the bottom of the hill, take a right on **Charles Street** (▷ 42). Stop at **Artù** (▷ 45) at 89 Charles Street for a panini, salad or pizza.

Afternoon Visit the antiques shops on Charles Street or visit **Nichols House** (▷ 39) or the **Museum of Afro-American History** (▷ 38).

Mid-afternoon Continue to the end of Charles Street, past the T station to the **Liberty Hotel** (▷ 112) for a drink in the Clink bar, and to admire the stunning architectural transformation of this former city jail.

Dinner Return to Charles Street for dinner at the **Beacon Hill Bistro** (▷ 45) or at the nearby **Upper Crust Pizzeria** (▷ 46) for authentic Italian pizzas.

Evening Take a 10-minute walk through **Boston Common** or the **Public Garden** (▷ 51), or a five-minute taxi ride around it, to the Theater District, to see a play in any of the city's excellent theaters.

DAY 2

Morning Start the day with a Parisian or American breakfast at **Brasserie JO** (▷84), opposite the Prudential Center, and continue along Huntington Avenue past Symphony Hall to the **Museum of Fine Arts** (▷70). It's easy to spend a day among its vast collections of French Impressionists, Egyptian artifacts and Early American decorative arts.

Mid-morning Walk along the Fens to the **Isabella Stewart Gardner Museum** (▷68–69) for a look at the home of a Boston legend and a stroll through her fabulous art collection.

Lunch Take the T to Harvard Square for lunch at **Casablanca** (▷97), a few steps from the station. Savor the creative Mediterranean cuisine and admire the mural depicting the cast of characters in the film *Casablanca*.

Afternoon Cross Harvard Yard to see the one-of-a-kind collection of glass flowers at the **Harvard Museum of Natural History** and a look at the Native American collections at the adjoining **Peabody Museum** (▷91).

Mid-afternoon Take a break from museums at **L. A. Burdick Chocolate** café (▷98) before continuing down Brattle Street for a look at the **Longfellow House** (▷92).

Dinner Head over to Harvard Square and dine at **Chez Henri** (▷97), a popular restaurant serving French Bistro cuisine with a zesty Cuban twist. Or try the funky **Upstairs on the Square** (▷98) with two choices, either casual comfort food or a traditional dinner menu with an eclectic atmosphere. Otherwise, dine at **Sandrine's** (▷98), where you can enjoy the Alsatian chef/owner's blend of French styles and seasonal local ingredients.

► ► ►

ESSENTIAL BOSTON TOP 25

Beacon Hill and Louisburg Square ▷ 24–25
Elegant residential district with some historic homes.

USS _Constitution_ and Charlestown ▷ 36–37
Naval museums and historic warships.

Trinity Church and Copley Square ▷ 76–77
New (John Hancock Tower) and old (Trinity Church) architecture rub shoulders in this square.

State House ▷ 35
The gold-domed landmark center of state government.

The South End ▷ 74–75
Lively, sought-after residential area with excellent restaurants and shops.

Prudential Center and Skywalk ▷ 73 An upscale shopping mall and stunning panoramic views from the 50th floor.

Paul Revere House ▷ 34 The legendary revolutionary's North End home and one of the few houses left from colonial America.

Old State House ▷ 32–33 Best museum for an overview of Boston's rich history.

Boston Athenaeum ▷ 50 A Boston institution, haunt of intellectuals and the country's first library.

Boston Common and Public Garden ▷ 51
Open-air playgrounds, ponds and gardens.

North End and the Old North Church ▷ 30–31
Historic church in the heart of Little Italy.

Newbury Street ▷ 72
Funky shops, luxury boutiques, pavement cafés and trendy restaurants.

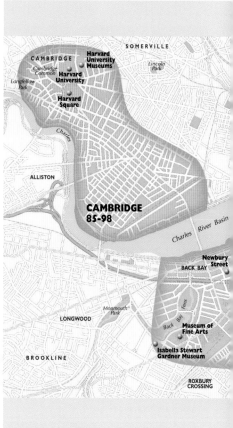

These pages are a quick guide to the Top 25, which are described in more detail later. Here they are listed alphabetically, and the tinted background shows which area they are in.

Boston Harbor Islands ▷ **102** Unspoiled havens of wildlife, historic forts and beaches.

Boston Public Library ▷ **66** Marbles, mosaics and murals in an oasis of tranquillity.

Commonwealth Avenue ▷ **67** Boston's grandest houses flank a green mall with noted statues.

Faneuil Hall and Marketplace ▷ **26** From first public meeting hall to food market and mall.

Harrison Gray Otis House ▷ **27** Restored Federal-style family home.

Harvard Square and Harvard University ▷ **88–89** Cafés, shops, street entertainers–the hub of student life.

Harvard University Museums ▷ **90–91** Four world-quality museums.

Institute of Contemporary Art ▷ **52** Cutting-edge architecture on the waterfront.

Isabella Stewart Gardner Museum ▷ **68–69** Superb works of art displayed in a palazzo setting.

JFK Library and Museum ▷ **103** Insight into JFK's life. His papers are held here.

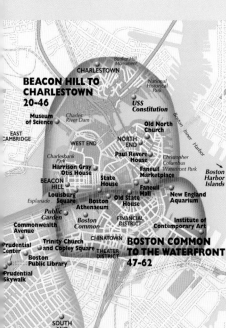

BEACON HILL TO CHARLESTOWN 20–46

BOSTON COMMON TO THE WATERFRONT 47–62

BACK BAY AND THE SOUTH END 63–84

New England Aquarium ▷ **53** A large collection–families will love this. Don't miss feeding time.

Museum of Science ▷ **28–29** Cutting-edge exhibits cover ocean waves to space travel.

Museum of Fine Arts ▷ **70–71** An exhaustive collection of treasures from around the globe.

ESSENTIAL BOSTON TOP 25

◄ ◄ ◄

9

Shopping

Some of Boston's best shopping areas are in the city's most attractive neighborhoods. One-of-a-kind shops selling clothes, books or antiques rub shoulders with outlets for contemporary crafts, innovative gifts and home accessories. Newbury Street is a joy, with its boutiques in lovely 19th-century brownstone buildings. People travel long distances to shop for clothes here, from top designer labels to the fabulously funky and the "gently used." With the great outdoors on the doorstep, many shops specialize in outdoors equipment and clothing.

Antiques

Like all of New England, Boston is good hunting ground for antiques. Clustered in and around Charles Street, at the foot of Beacon Hill, are dozens of shops. Most are specialists, selling oriental rugs, furniture, porcelain, silver or antique maps for serious money. Even if you can't afford to buy, it's a pleasure to browse. In Cambridge, hundreds of dealers in two large markets offer less expensive collectibles, alongside furniture, silverware and other antiques.

Books

Boston has a plethora of bookshops—new, used and antiquarian—particularly around Harvard Square. Whether you're looking for a coffee-table book on Boston to take back home, or something rare and erudite, you can browse undisturbed until 11pm in some stores.

ONLY IN BOSTON

Baked beans were invented in Boston by early colonists, who cooked them in molasses. Today, red Boston beans (albeit in candy form) are sold on souvenir stands. The lobster shows up in the usual touristy guises, from fridge magnets to pencil tops and notebooks. As for T-shirts, sweatshirts and baseball caps, they bear logos of local universities, like Harvard, and local teams, including the Patriots, the Bruins, the Celtics and, of course, 2004 and 2007 World Series winners, the Red Sox.

Clockwise from top left: Downtown Crossing; colorful handmade glass; shop sign; Harvard Book

Boutiques

Many of the small independent stores in Back Bay, Beacon Hill, the South End and Cambridge brim with interesting finds—from pottery made by Boston artists and soaps made by local beauty companies to hand-knit sweaters. Even on Newbury Street, which at first glance seems to be full of pricey international brands, you'll find local businesses tucked in among the heavy hitters.

Outlet Shopping

Some of New England's big outlets—where clothes, shoes and household goods are available at discounts of up to 65 percent—are within an hour of central Boston. They make a tempting day trip if you get a buzz from finding a bargain.

Farmers' Markets

At the farmers' markets that start up in spring in Copley Square (Tuesday, Friday), South Station (Thursday) and Harvard Square (Tuesday, Friday), you can find all the goodies available at roadside farm stands around rural areas of New England—fresh fruits, ice cream, maple syrup, cheese and honey, among other things. Maple-cream candy (sweets) and plastic jugs of maple syrup make easy-to-pack souvenirs and gifts.

Contemporary Crafts

The best (and easy-to-find) places to shop for contemporary crafts are in Newbury and Charles streets, as well as in Cambridge and the South End.

Store; Faneuil Hall Marketplace; shop sign in Beacon Hill

UNIQUELY BOSTON

Shopping is one of the favorite activities for visitors to Boston, with some tourism surveys ranking shopping popularity higher than visiting the museums and historic attractions. Clothing costing less than $175 is exempt from the 6.25 percent Massachusetts sales tax. Good shopping areas are located in Back Bay and South End, Beacon Hill and Faneuil Hall, Downtown and Cambridge.

Shopping by Theme

You'll find all sorts of shops in Boston. On this page they are listed by theme with cross references to more detailed information.

ANTIQUES

Cambridge Antique Market (▷ 94)
Charles Street (▷ panel, 42)
Danish Country Antiques (▷ 41)

BOOKS AND MAPS

Brattle Bookshop (▷ 58)
Curious George Goes to WordsWorth (▷ 94)
Globe Corner Bookstore (▷ 94)
Grolier Poetry Bookshop (▷ 94)
Harvard Bookstore (▷ 94)
Harvard Coop (▷ 94)
Schoenhof's Foreign Books (▷ 95)

FOR CHILDREN

Build-A-Bear Workshop (▷ 41)
Curious George Goes to WordsWorth (▷ 94)
Harvard Coop (▷ 94)
The Red Wagon (▷ 42)
Stellabella Toys (▷ 95)

CLOTHES

1154 Lill Studio (▷ 80)
Alan Bilzerian (▷ 80)
American Apparel (▷ 80)
Emporio Armani (▷ 80)
Filene's Basement (▷ 80)
Gretta Luxe (▷ 80)
Holiday Boutique (▷ 42)
Linens on the Hill (▷ 42)
Louis Boston (▷ 58)
Marc Jacobs (▷ 81)
Mint Julep (▷ 95)
Nomad (▷ 95)
St. John Boutique (▷ 58)
Second Time Around (▷ 81)
Tess & Carlos (▷ 95)
Urban Outfitters (▷ 95)
Via Vai (▷ 95)
Wish Boutique (▷ 42)

CRAFTS

Artful Hand (▷ 80)
Beadworks (▷ 94)
Cambridge Artists' Cooperative (▷ 94)

DISTRICTS AND MALLS

Barneys New York (▷ 80)
CambridgeSide Galleria (▷ 41)
Charles Street (▷ panel, 42)
Downtown Crossing (▷ 58)
Harvard Square (▷ 94)
Newbury Street (▷ panel, 81)
Prudential Center (▷ 81)

FOODS

Beacon Hill Chocolates (▷ 41)
Cardullo's (▷ 94)
Hidden Sweets (▷ 95)
Savenor's (▷ 42)

GIFTS/HOUSEHOLD

Abodeon (▷ 94)
Black Ink (▷ 41)
Boston Pewter Company (▷ 41)
Bostonian Society Museum Shop (▷ 41)
Bromfield Pen Shop (▷ 58)
Brookstone (▷ 80)
Copley Flair (▷ 41)
Crate & Barrell (▷ 41)
Eugene Galleries (▷ 41)
Flat of the Hill (▷ 42)
Four Preppy Paws (▷ 42)
Geoclassics (▷ 42)
Good, Inc (▷ 42)
The ICA Store (▷ 58)
Koo de Kir (▷ 42)
Leavitt & Pierce Inc. (▷ 95)
Lekker (▷ 80)
Lush (▷ 81)
Matsu (▷ 81)
MDF (▷ 95)
Museum of Fine Arts Gift Shop (▷ 42)
Pierre Deux (▷ 81)
Pottery Barn (▷ 81)
Simon Pearce (▷ 81)
Williams-Sonoma (▷ 81)

MUSIC

Newbury Comics (▷ 81, 95)

OUTDOOR GEAR

Allen Edmonds (▷ 80)
Coach (▷ 41)
Foot Paths (▷ 58)
Hilton's Tent City (▷ 42)
Niketown (▷ 81)
Skechers (▷ 58)
Tannery (▷ 58)

Boston by Night

Although Boston's not a city that never sleeps, you'll still find evening diversions aplenty.

Illuminations
For magical views of Boston's skyline visit the Prudential Skywalk, or cross over the Charles River to Cambridge on the T. Memorial Drive, between Longfellow and Harvard bridges, is a good spot to view the floodlit downtown sky-scrapers. In winter, trees twinkle with lights.

People-Watching
One of the liveliest spots for people-watching is the North End, where Italian music fills the narrow streets and restaurants hum with the chatter of Italian families. On Newbury Street people sit outdoors in cafés surveying the pedestrian parade.

Clubs and Bars
Boston club kids head for Lansdowne Street, near Kenmore Square. For cocktails and to catch the latest music, young professionals go to Boylston Place, a little alley in the Theater District. The RegattaBar (▷ 97) on Harvard Square is one of the best-known jazz venues in the east.

Late-Night Restaurants
Most restaurants do not serve after 10pm, but you could try Chinatown, where many places stay open until 4am. In the South End, several restaurants serve until 1am on weekends.

From top: Faneuil Hall; Fenway Park; Chinatown; nightclub; Hatch Shell

---

LIVE ENTERTAINMENT

Entertainment ranges from the Boston Symphony, Boston Ballet and traveling Broadway shows to rock concerts, avant-garde dance and student theater. In summer, see free movies, concerts and theater on outdoor stages. There are summer concerts at Hatch Shell (▷ 83), as well as free movies. Watch for free band concerts on City Hall Plaza (☎ 617/635-4505) in July and August, and for performances by Boston Landmarks Orchestra (☎ 617/520-2200; www.landmarksorchestra. org).

Eating Out

Once known primarily as the home of beans and cod, Boston has blossomed into a first-rate culinary center.

Eclectic Menus
Where fried seafood and traditional Yankee fare once dominated menus, they're now offered alongside local seafood, with ceviche and mignonette-splashed oysters appearing regularly. Boston's restaurants are some of the country's best, from the snazzy bar-restaurants of Back Bay to its four-star New American ones.

Bistros
In general, bistros are the most popular genre of restaurant around town; they tend to show up as hip, candlelit spots on Newbury Street or family-run joints in the South End. What they have in common is a sophisticated but unpretentious quality, and often excellent food.

Elegant Dining
A level or two up in price and service, you'll find sophisticated dishes made by Boston's most admired chefs, many of whom have been in the city for years.

Ethnic Restaurants
Boston's ethnic cuisines go beyond Chinatown and the North End Italian neighborhood. In Cambridge, the Portuguese enclave is around Inman Square, and several Irish pubs are nearby. Elsewhere in the city are Ethiopian, Asian and Latin American restaurants.

OPENING TIMES

Restaurant times vary slightly all over the city, but most open for dinner between 5 and 6pm and a few serve dinner until 11pm or midnight, and offer an abridged menu if they happen to house a bar. Many of the trendier restaurants do not serve breakfast or lunch, and some are not open at all on Monday. Reservations are a must at any but the most casual places, but particularly for popular eating destinations like Back Bay and the South End.

From top: Newbury Street café; Faneuil Hall Marketplace; outdoor dining; Chinatown

Restaurants by Cuisine

There are restaurants to suit all tastes and budgets in Boston. On this page they are listed by cuisine. For a more detailed description of each restaurant, see Boston by Area.

AMERICAN AND MEXICAN

Border Café (▷ 97)
Café Fleuri (▷ 61)
Craigie on Main (▷ 98)
Grill 23 & Bar (▷ 61)
Hungry I (▷ 45)
Icarus (▷ 84)
Mr. Bartley's Burger Cottage (▷ 98)
Plaza III, The Kansas City Steakhouse (▷ 46)
Slugger's Dugout (▷ 46)
Union Bar & Grille (▷ 84)

ASIAN AND MIDDLE EASTERN

Chau Chow City (▷ 61)
Haru (▷ 84)
Lala Rokh (▷ 45)
New Shanghai (▷ 62)
Sultan's Kitchen (▷ 46)

BOSTON'S BEST

Aura (▷ 61)
The Bristol Lounge (▷ 61)
Chez Henri (▷ 97)
Clio (▷ 84)
Durgin Park (▷ 45)
L'Espalier (▷ 84)
Hamersley's Bistro (▷ 84)
Meritage (▷ 62)
No. 9 Park (▷ 46)
Om Restaurant & Lounge (▷ 98)
Radius (▷ 62)
Union Oyster House (▷ 46)
Upstairs on the Square (▷ 98)

BRUNCH

The Blue Room (▷ 97)
Henrietta's Table (▷ panel, 98)
Sel de la Terre (▷ 62)

COFFEE AND SNACKS

Caffè Vittoria (▷ 45)
Christina's (▷ 98)
Flour Bakery (▷ panel, 84)
Hi-Rise (▷ 98)
L. A. Burdick Chocolate (▷ 98)
Napoli Pastry Shop (▷ 46)

FRENCH, ITALIAN AND MEDITERRANEAN

Antico Forno (▷ 45)
Artù (▷ 45)
Beacon Hill Bistro (▷ 45)
Bistro du Midi (▷ 61)
Brasserie Jo (▷ 84)
Cantina Italiana (▷ 45)
Casa Romero (▷ 84)
La Famiglia Giorgio's Restaurant (▷ 45)
Mamma Maria (▷ 46)
Petit Robert Bistro (▷ 84)
Prezza (▷ 46)
Rialto (▷ 98)
Sandrine's (▷ 98)
Teatro (▷ 62)
Upper Crust Pizzeria (▷ 46)
Via Matta (▷ 62)

SEAFOOD

Barking Crab (▷ 61)
Kingfish Hall (▷ 45)
Legal Sea Foods (▷ 98)
Legal Test Kitchen (▷ 62)
New Jumbo Seafood (▷ 62)
Rowes Wharf Sea Grille (▷ 62)

VEGETARIAN

Buddha's Delight (▷ panel, 62)
Casablanca (▷ 97)
Milk Street Café (▷ panel, 62)

If You Like...

However you'd like to spend your time in Boston, these top suggestions should help you tailor your ideal visit. Each suggestion has a fuller write-up elsewhere in the book.

LAZY MORNINGS

Take a stroll through the Public Garden (▷ 51).
Sip a coffee and people-watch from a table in Napoli Pastry (▷ 46) in the North End.
Walk along the Charles River Esplanade, the scenic pathway stretching along the river (▷ 78).
Go whale-watching out of Boston Harbor from the Aquarium (▷ 53).

SPECIALIST SHOPPING

Find the perfect shirt at a Newbury Street boutique (▷ 72).
Dig into some of the city's hottest music at Newbury Comics (▷ 81).
Act wonderfully childish at Curious George Goes to WordsWorth children's bookstore (▷ 94).
Find one-of-a-kind crafts and handmade jewelry at the ICA Store (▷ 58).
Discover new specialty cheeses and meats at Savenor's Market (▷ 42).

The swan boats in Boston Public Garden and trees on Charles River Esplanade (above)

BOSTON CULTURE

At Isabella Stewart Gardner Museum (▷ 68) see the stunning collection of international art in an attractive mansion.
View world-class collections at the Museum of Fine Arts (▷ 70): European and American art; Egyptian, Chinese and Classical artifacts.
Visit Trinity Church (▷ 76): A beautiful church founded before the Revolution.
Listen to the renowned Boston Symphony Orchestra at Symphony Hall (▷ 83).

The neo-Romanesque Trinity Church reflected in the I. M. Pei-designed John Hancock Tower (above right); Boston Symphony Orchestra performing in the Symphony Hall (right)

Spectacular view of Boston at night (below)

SKYSCRAPERS

Explore Prudential Tower (▷ 73): Shops, restaurants and souvenirs.

Admire the John Hancock Tower (▷ 77): I. M. Pei & Partners designed this glass-enclosed building, which reflects the buildings surrounding it.

Ascend Custom House Tower (▷ 38) for the great views from this skyscraper-turned-hotel.

COMMUNING WITH NATURE

Relax in the Public Garden (▷ 51). Manicured and bustling, it's filled with citydwellers and tourists alike.

Amble through Back Bay Fens (▷ 78): a string of parks, once a shallow bay.

Watch the boats go by in Christopher Columbus Waterfront Park (▷ 38).

Experience the 265 acres (106ha) of lilac blooms, roses and rare Asian trees at Arnold Arboretum (▷ 104) in Cambridge.

A STATUE TRAIL

See a dramatic ode to the first all-black regiment to fight in the Civil War (▷ 56): Robert Gould Shaw Memorial in Boston Common.

Make Way for the Ducklings: A charming tribute to Robert McCloskey's children's book, located in the Public Garden (▷ 51).

Honor three women who contributed to Boston's history—Abigail Adams, Lucy Stone and Phillis Wheatley at the Boston Women's Memorial on Commonwealth Avenue (▷ 67).

White swan in the Public Garden (above middle); Arnold Arboretum (above)

Bronze statue in the Public Garden (left), part of the collection inspired by Robert McCloskey's children's story "Make Way for the Ducklings"

KEEPING THE CHILDREN OCCUPIED

The Children's Museum (below); the Museum of Fine Arts (below middle)

Enjoy a fun, hands-on day of learning at the Museum of Science (▷28).
Find interactive exhibits on bubble-making, how televisions work and more at the Children's Museum (▷54).
Take a dramatic, spiral trip around a glowing tank full of sea creatures at the New England Aquarium (▷53).

BEING ENTERTAINED

Get in on the act: American Repertory Theatre (▷96) is Harvard's innovative and ambitious production house.
Watch a highly regarded company performing classical and contemporary productions at José Mateo's Ballet Theatre (▷96).

LOOKING FOR A BARGAIN

Visit Harvard's three art museums (The Sackler, Fogg and Busch-Reisinger, ▷91) free of charge on Saturday morning until noon.
At the Museum of Fine Arts, pay what you like for entry on Wednesday nights after 4pm (▷70).
Find half-price theater tickets the day of a performance at BosTix booths (▷panel, 59) at Faneuil Hall Marketplace and Copley Square.

The 18th-century Faneuil Hall (above)

ENJOYING NEW ENGLAND SEAFOOD

Head to Legal Sea Foods, (▷98) a local chain known for fresh lobsters and clam chowder.
Be more daring and head for Legal Test Kitchen (▷62) for international takes on the freshest seafood.

Delicious Pacific shrimp (right)

Boston by Area

Sights	24–39
Walk	40
Shopping	41–42
Entertainment and Nightlife	43
Restaurants	45–46

BEACON HILL TO CHARLESTOWN

Sights	50–56
Walk	57
Shopping	58
Entertainment and Nightlife	59–60
Restaurants	61–62

BOSTON COMMON TO THE WATERFRONT

Sights	66–78
Walk	79
Shopping	80–81
Entertainment and Nightlife	82–83
Restaurants	84

BACK BAY AND THE SOUTH END

Sights	89–92
Walk	93
Shopping	94–95
Entertainment and Nightlife	96–97
Restaurants	97–98

CAMBRIDGE

Sights	102–104
Excursions	105–106

FARTHER AFIELD

This neighborhood merges historic buildings and monuments with skyscrapers.

Sights	24–39	Top 25	**TOP 25**
Walk	40	Beacon Hill and Louisburg Square ▷ **24**	
Shopping	41–42	Faneuil Hall and Marketplace ▷ **26**	
		Harrison Gray Otis House ▷ **27**	
Entertainment and Nightlife	43	Museum of Science ▷ **28**	
		North End and Old North Church ▷ **30**	
Restaurants	45–46	Old State House ▷ **32**	
		Paul Revere House ▷ **34**	
		State House ▷ **35**	
		USS *Constitution* and Charlestown ▷ **36**	

Beacon Hill to Charlestown

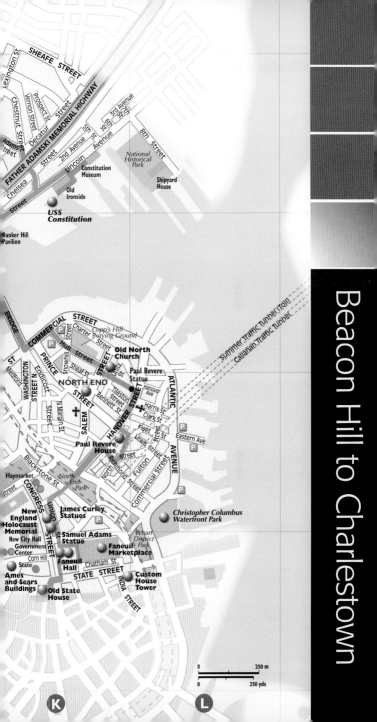

SHEAFE STREET

Lexington St

Chestnut Street

Vernon Street

Prospect St.

Decatur Street

Adams Street

Chelsea Street

FATHER ADAMSKI MEMORIAL HIGHWAY

2nd Avenue

3rd Avenue

5th St.

2nd St.

Avenue

8th Street

Lincoln Street

National Historical Park

Constitution Museum

Shipyard House

Old Ironside

USS Constitution

Bunker Hill Pavilion

Summer Traffic Tunnel (Toll)

Callahan Traffic Tunnel

BRIDGE ST

COMMERCIAL STREET

Charter Street

Copp's Hill Burying Ground

Hull Street

Snowhill Street

PRINCE STREET

WASHINGTON STREET N

Medford Street

Endicott St.

Sheaf St.

SALEM STREET

N Margin St.

Old North Church

Union St.

Tileston Street

Bennett Street

Paul Revere Statue

Hanover Ave

Harris St.

Clark St.

HANOVER STREET

ATLANTIC

Fleet Street

Lewis Street

Eastern Ave

NORTH END

Paul Revere House

North Street

Richmond Street

Fulton Street

Commercial Street

AVENUE

Blackstone St.

Haymarket

North End Park

CONGRESS STREET

Union St.

New England Holocaust Memorial

James Curley Statues

New City Hall
Government Center

Samuel Adams Statue

Corn Hill

Faneuil Hall

Chatham St.

Faneuil Marketplace

Wharf District Park

Christopher Columbus Waterfront Park

Ames and Sears Buildings

State

Old State House

STATE STREET

INDIA STREET

Custom House Tower

0 — 250 m

0 — 250 yds

K   L

Beacon Hill to Charlestown

Beacon Hill and Louisburg Square

HIGHLIGHTS

● Louisburg Square
● Pinckney Street and its view of Charles River
● Nichols House Museum
● Charles Street shops and restaurants

BOSTON BRAHMINS

● Oliver Wendell Holmes called those Bostonians who could trace their origins to the wealthy merchants of the 18th and 19th centuries, Brahmins after the high-ranking Hindu caste.

Beacon Hill is an enclave of elegant redbrick houses in a leafy maze of steep streets and narrow, cobbled lanes—it is a delightful area to explore on foot.

Brahmin stronghold After the opening of the State House on its southern slope, Beacon Hill was developed as a prestigious residential area by entrepreneurs including Boston's famous architect Charles Bulfinch. Boston's top families swiftly moved in. Rich as they were, these "Brahmins" were also the personification of Puritan reserve. Showiness was taboo, so the houses were restrained, with elegant doorways and ironwork gracing plain brick facades.

Perfectly preserved To get the magic of it all, choose a sunny day and just wander, noting the

Clockwise from left: Mount Vernon Street; leafy Louisburg Square; cobbled Acorn Street in Beacon Hill; a redbrick building in the Beacon Hill district; autumn leaves; De Luca's Market on Charles Street

pillared porticoes, genteel fanlights and flowery window boxes. A walk through Beacon Hill leads you to some of the city's most treasured corners, including Mount Vernon Street, Chestnut Street, tiny Acorn Street and, best of all, Louisburg Square. Here Bulfinch's lovely bow fronts look onto a central garden reminiscent of a European square. Notice how the street lamps are lighted all day and look for the purple window panes: Manganese oxide in a batch of glass reacted with sunlight to produce discolored but now highly prized and very distinctive panes. To see inside a Beacon Hill home, visit the Nichols House Museum. On the hill's north slope from Pinckney Street down to Cambridge Street, the houses are smaller and more varied. It has several important sites in the history of Boston's African-American community, including the African Meeting House.

THE BASICS

H5

⊠ Bounded by Beacon Street, Embankment Road, Cambridge Street, Bowdoin Street

🍴 Choice in Charles Street

🚇 Park Street, Charles/MGH, Arlington, Bowdoin (closed Sat)

♿ Steep hills, some uneven surfaces

❓ Historic New England tours of Beacon Hill; Black Heritage Trail: See Museum of Afro-American History (▷ 38)

Faneuil Hall and Marketplace

A statue and an avenue of trees in front of Faneuil Hall (left); market stand (right)

THE BASICS

www.faneuilhallmarket
place.com

🔳 K5

✉ Congress Street

☎ 617/242-5642

🕐 Great Hall: 9–5
(when not in use)

🍴 A plethora of eating
places

🚇 State, Aquarium,
Government Center

♿ Good

🎫 Great Hall: free

❓ Great Hall: 15-min talk
every half-hour

HIGHLIGHTS

● Great Hall
● Grasshopper weathervane
on the roof
● Quincy's granite market
buildings
● Street entertainers
● Food vendors in Quincy
Market

Faneuil Hall is a landmark for all Americans, the place where the iniquities of the British government were first debated in the 1770s. Now, its market-place is a landmark for visitors.

"Cradle of Liberty" A wealthy trader of Huguenot origins, Peter Faneuil, presented the town with a market hall with a meeting room above. Ever since, the lower hall has been a market and the galleried upper hall has been a place for public gatherings. In the 1700s, because the town meetings frequently discussed the problems with Britain that led up to the revolution and independence, Faneuil Hall became known as America's "Cradle of Liberty." Since then national issues, from the abolition of slavery to the Vietnam War, have been aired here. The room bears all the trademarks of Charles Bulfinch, the architect who built so much of Boston. He expanded the hall in 1805.

Quincy's marketplace Despite the Bulfinch expansion, more space was soon needed. In 1826, with some inspired town planning that radically changed Boston's waterfront, mayor Josiah Quincy filled in Town Dock and built over the wharves, providing a granite market hall flanked by granite warehouses. These were a wholesale food market until the 1960s. In the 1970s the area was renovated and revitalized, and is now the city's main tourist attraction (known as either Faneuil Hall Marketplace or Quincy Market) with dozens of shops, pushcarts, stands, eating places and street entertainers.

The elegant dining room (right) of Harrison Gray Otis House (left)

TOP 25

Harrison Gray Otis House

This is Boston's only remaining Federal-style mansion. Meticulously restored in its every detail, the gracious interior is an accurate representation of how the upper classes lived in the 19th century.

Otis and Bulfinch One of the leading lights in post-Revolutionary Boston politics was the lawyer Harrison Gray Otis (1765–1844), long-standing friend of architect Charles Bulfinch. In 1796 he commissioned Bulfinch to build him this grand mansion in what was then the elegant area of Bowdoin Square. The structure's very restrained, very proper, brick facade is typical of what became known as the Federal style. Five years later, Bulfinch built Otis an even bigger house on newly developed Beacon Hill (▷ 24–25), to which all the wealthy were migrating. By the 1830s the Otis home had become a boarding house.

Authenticity In 1916 the Society for the Preservation of New England Antiquities, now Historic New England, bought the property as its headquarters. Accuracy and authenticity being its hallmarks, the organization has restored the interior with reproduction wallpapers and paint colors (some surprisingly bright) based on paint analysis. Otis and his wife, Sally, were lavish entertainers and the parlor, dining room and drawing room, furnished in high Federal style, provide an insight into social manners of the day, while bedrooms, kitchens and servant quarters give you a glimpse of family life. One upstairs room shows the mansion as it looked when it was a boarding house.

THE BASICS

www.historicnewengland.org

⊞ J4

✉ 141 Cambridge Street

☎ 617/227-3956

🕐 Wed–Sun 11–4.30. Tours on the hour and half hour

🍴 None

🚇 Bowdoin (closed Sat), Charles/MGH, Government Center

♿ Wheelchairs first floor only

💵 Moderate. Historic New England members free

❓ Walking tours of Beacon Hill mid-May to mid-Oct, Sat (call ahead). Shop

HIGHLIGHTS

● Bulfinch Federal design
● Reproductions of original wallpaper
● Yellow and turquoise paints
● Federal-era furniture

Museum of Science

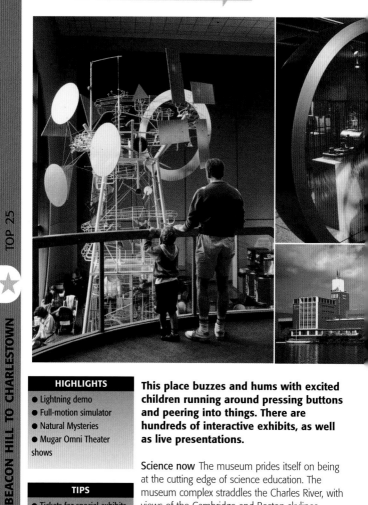

- Lightning demo
- Full-motion simulator
- Natural Mysteries
- Mugar Omni Theater shows

TIPS

- Tickets for special exhibits often sell out during school vacation weeks. Buy in advance online.
- Arrive at least a half-hour early for Omni Theater shows to get the best seats.

This place buzzes and hums with excited children running around pressing buttons and peering into things. There are hundreds of interactive exhibits, as well as live presentations.

Science now The museum prides itself on being at the cutting edge of science education. The museum complex straddles the Charles River, with views of the Cambridge and Boston skylines.

"It's awesome" Don't miss the dramatic indoor lightning demos in the Theater of Electricity, where the world's largest Van de Graaff generator creates 2.5 million volts of electricity. Between shows, take part in the popular Virtual Volleyball exhibit. Close by, peer into the mouth of a T-Rex, modeled to reflect the latest paleontological theories.

Clockwise from far left: A father and son examine an exhibit at the museum; the blur of the fast-spinning wheels of a steam-powered engine; a crowded show in the Mugar Omni Theater; a model space station; a giant locust model; the museum from the outside reflected in the Charles River

A large portion of the museum has rotating special exhibits, featuring popular topics such as the magical world of Harry Potter, or cutting-edge 3D films about the human body. The Simulator Experience is a full-motion simulator excursion that takes you through space, the deep sea and along the path of a water molecule. Other popular exhibits include the Natural Mysteries, where you learn about scientific classification from collections of skulls, animal tracks, shells and more. There are also presentations at the Science Live! Stage.

Mugar Omni Theater and the Planetarium Lie back and be enveloped in the sight and sound of an IMAX movie in the five-story screen of the Mugar Omni Theater. Multimedia presentations at the Charles Hayden Planetarium cover astronomical subjects. Evening laser shows take place here.

THE BASICS

www.mos.org

➕ H3

✉ Science Park

☎ 617/723-2500

🕐 Jul 5–Labor Day Sat–Thu 9–7, Fri 9–9. Labor Day– Jul 4 Sat–Thu 9–5, Fri 9–9. Extended hours over school holidays

🍴 Three on premises

Ⓢ Science Park

♿ Excellent. Sight- and hearing-impaired facilities

💲 Expensive. Separate tickets for Planetarium, Laser Show, Omni Theater. Combination ticket discounts. Boston CityPass applies

❓ Good shop

North End and Old North Church

HIGHLIGHTS

● Paul Revere House
(▷ 34)
● Old North Church Steeple
● Copp's Hill Burying
Ground (▷ opposite)
● Feast-day processions
● Italian groceries, coffee
shops and restaurants

TIP

● The North End explodes
with life and color in late
August for the Feast of
St. Anthony.

**The North End is Boston's oldest and
most spirited district. This is where
the British colonists settled in the 17th
century, and now, after various ups and
downs, it is a lively Italian quarter.**

Little Italy The North End is separated from the
rest of Boston by an area that was once a major
highway, and is now a park. When the colonists
arrived it was also all but cut off, surrounded then
by water at the end of a narrow peninsula. The
colonists' erratic street plan survives, but the only
building from the 17th century is Paul Revere
House. Once the elite had moved to Beacon Hill
in the early 19th century, the area played host to
waves of immigrants, first the Irish, then East
Europeans and Portuguese and finally Italians who
have given the area its current flavor.

The equestrian statue of Paul Revere with St. Stephen's Church beyond (left); Old North Church is now overshadowed by office buildings (middle); the decorative sign that welcomes visitors to North End (right)

Paul Revere Mall On Hanover Street, opposite St. Stephen's Church, the mall connects the North End's main street to Old North Church. This tree-shaded park is James Rego Square, but locals call it the Prado. Standing at one end is a bronze equestrian statue of Paul Revere (▷ panel, 125).

Old North Church It was from Old North that Revere's signal was given to the patriots in Charlestown that the British were on their way to Lexington where, the next day, the first battle of the War of Independence took place.

Copp's Hill Burying Ground Up the hill in front of Old North Church is a former Native American lookout point. In 1659 it became a burying ground, visited now for its rows of slate and stone headstones, many carved with winged skulls.

THE BASICS

✚ K4/K3
✉ Bounded by Commercial Street and Expressway
🕐 Old North Church: daily. Closed Mon Jan–Feb. Steeple: Jun–Oct daily
🍴 Plenty around Hanover and Salem streets
🚇 Haymarket, North Station, Aquarium, State
♿ Some hills and uneven sidewalks (pavements)

Old State House

HIGHLIGHTS

● Lion and unicorn
● Balcony from which the Declaration of Independence was read
● Exhibit showing topographical changes

TIPS

● Check the website for the latest events program.
● Don't miss the tiny phial of tea leaves saved from the Boston Tea Party.
● Light up the topographical map to see how much of Boston is built on landfill.

This is the city's oldest public building, once the seat of British colonial government. Surrounded by taller—but far less significant—buildings, it seems so tiny now. It holds a first-rate museum.

Colonial capital Built in 1713 to replace an earlier Town House, the Old State House was the British governor's seat of office, home to the judicial court and to the Massachusetts Assembly. As such it was the scene of many a confrontation between the colonists and their rulers. It was here that James Otis railed against the "tyranny of taxation without representation" and it was under the balcony at the east end that the "Boston Massacre" took place in 1770: Five colonists were killed in a clash with British soldiers, a key event in the years leading up to the Revolution. From the

The Puritan interior of the Old State House (left) and the lion and unicorn on the east front (right)

same balcony, the Declaration of Independence was read on July 18, 1776, and is still read every July 4. At this point the gilded lion and unicorn on the east front, symbols of the British Crown, were destroyed. From 1780 until 1798, this was the Massachusetts State House. For most of the 19th century it was used for commercial purposes, gradually falling into disrepair until the Bostonian Society was founded in 1881 to restore it. The lion and the unicorn were returned to their place, balanced now by the American eagle and the Massachusetts seal.

A Museum of Boston The building is now home to the Bostonian Society's excellent museum, which traces the city's topographical, political, economic and social history, with a fine collection of maritime art and revolutionary memorabilia.

THE BASICS

www.bostonhistory.org
+ K5
✉ 206 Washington Street
☎ 617/720-1713
🕐 Daily 9–5 (Jan till 4, Jul–Aug till 6)
🍴 Nearby
Ⓢ State, Government Center, Downtown Crossing
♿ No access to upper floor
💰 Inexpensive
❓ Shop

Paul Revere House

TOP 25

The bedroom (left) in Paul Revere House and views of the exterior (middle and right)

THE BASICS

www.paulreverehouse.org
K4
19 North Square
617/523-2338
Nov to mid-Apr daily 9.30–4.15; mid-Apr to Oct daily 9.30–5.15. Jan–Mar closed Mon
Nearby
Government Center, State, Aquarium, Haymarket
Wheelchair access first floor only
Inexpensive
Tours of early Georgian Pierce/Hichborn House

HIGHLIGHTS

- Revere's own account of his ride
- Period furnishings

TIPS

- Avoid the house on spring and fall (autumn) afternoons, when it is often overrun by school groups.
- Check ahead for the appearances by costumed interpreters.

This house is all that remains of the 17th-century settlement in today's North End. Not only is it Boston's oldest building, it was home to its most celebrated revolutionary, Paul Revere.

The early years The steep-gabled clapboard house that we see today was built in about 1680. Like most houses of the period, it had two rooms on each of its two floors but the positioning of the main staircase at the side of the building, making the rooms larger than normal, was unusual. By 1770, when the silversmith and engraver Paul Revere came to live here, significant alterations had been made, notably the addition of a third floor and a two-story extension at the back. The family lived here during the Revolution, so it was from here that Revere set out on that famous midnight ride (▷ panel, 125). In 1800, after the family sold the house, it became a rooming house, with stores and factory premises on the lower floor. Threatened with demolition in 1902, it was saved by Revere's great-grandson, restored to something like its origins and became a museum.

The house today The basic timber skeleton of the house is the original, but the exterior clapboarding, the windows and most of what you see inside are replacements. Go through the kitchen into the living room, furnished in period style. Upstairs, the main bedroom is an elegantly furnished room, which would have doubled as a parlor. In the other room, note the ingenious folding bed and its traditional woven cover.

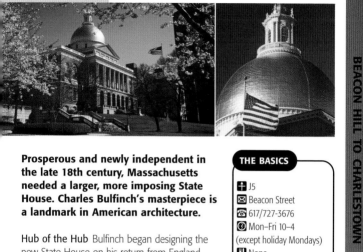

State House (left) with its gleaming gold-leaf dome (right)

State House

Prosperous and newly independent in the late 18th century, Massachusetts needed a larger, more imposing State House. Charles Bulfinch's masterpiece is a landmark in American architecture.

Hub of the Hub Bulfinch began designing the new State House on his return from England, much influenced by Robert Adam's Renaissance style. Construction began in 1795 on a prominent piece of Beacon Hill land. Cut off in your mind's eye the side wings (an early 20th-century addition), and focus on Bulfinch's dignified two-story portico and the glistening dome. Its original shingles were covered in copper from the foundry of Paul Revere when the roof began to leak, and the gold leaf was added in 1874. Until skyscrapers arrived, it dominated the city skyline.

Seat of government Start your tour in the columned Doric Hall. From here pass through the marble Nurses' Hall and note Bela Pratt's memorial to Civil War nurses. The Italian marble floor in the Hall of Flags was laid by immigrants from Italy. Featured in the stained-glass skylight are the seals of the original 13 states. Up the staircase is the House of Representatives chamber. Here, the Sacred Cod, a symbol of the importance of the fishing industry and a lucky mascot, must hang whenever the 160 state representatives are in session. The dignified barrel-vaulted and Ionic-columned Senate Reception Room is Bulfinch's, as is the Senate Chamber, where 40 senators debate beneath a graceful sunburst dome.

THE BASICS

* J5
* Beacon Street
* 617/727-3676
* Mon–Fri 10–4 (except holiday Mondays)
* None
* Park Street
* Partial wheelchair access
* Free
* Regular tours (45 min); last tour 3.30. It is advisable to call in advance to reserve a guided tour

HIGHLIGHTS

* Gold dome (regilded in 1997 with 22 carat gold leaf)
* Sacred Cod
* Senate Reception Room
* Senate Chamber
* JFK statue

TIP

* To enter the State House for tours use the side entrance on Bowdoin Street.

USS *Constitution* and Charlestown

HIGHLIGHTS

● Museum: details of a sailor's daily diet and duties
● USS *Constitution*: cramped lower deck

TIPS

● If you are walking the Freedom Trail from Boston, get here by 3pm to take a tour of the ship.
● Kids will love the top floor of the museum, where they can fire ships' cannons in interactive games.

"Old Ironsides," as she is widely known by schoolchildren, is the oldest commissioned warship afloat in the world. More than 200 years old, she is moored in the Charlestown Navy Yard.

The Navy Yard From 1800 to 1974 the Charlestown Navy Yard played an important role building, repairing and supplying Navy warships. Its mission now is to interpret the history of naval shipbuilding. Representing the ships built here are USS *Constitution* and the World War II destroyer USS *Cassin Young*, both of which may be boarded. The old granite Building 22 now houses the USS *Constitution* Museum, where journals and objects record the frigate's 200-year career in war and peace and give a picture of life aboard. Also open is the Commandant's House.

Clockwise from far left: Gleaming cannons on the restored frigate USS Constitution, "Old Ironsides"; the world's oldest commissioned battleship, at dock in Charlestown Navy Yard; detail of the craftsmanship and rigging that have kept this venerable vessel afloat; view of the prow and masts; rigging winch

THE BASICS

www.history.navy.mil/ussconstitution

www.nps.gov/bost

K2/J2

Charlestown Navy Yard

Navy Yard Visitor Center: 617/242-5601

USS *Constitution* Museum: mid-Apr to mid-Oct 9–6; mid-Oct to mid-Apr 10–5. USS *Constitution*: Apr–Oct Tue–Sun 10–6; Nov–Mar Thu–Sat 10–4. USS *Cassin Young*: daily 12–3 (Jul–Aug 10–5), weather permitting; guided tours daily 11, 2. Bunker Hill Monument: daily 9–4.30 (till 5.30 Jul–Aug). Bunker Hill Museum: daily 9–5 (till 6 Jul–Aug)

In the Navy Yard

North Station or Community College, then 15-min walk

MBTA Water Shuttle from Long Wharf

All wheelchair accessible except USS *Cassin Young*

All free except USS *Constitution* Museum (donation)

The Bunker Hill Pavilion's diorama, "The Battle of Bunker Hill," tells the story of the battle. The Bunker Hill Monument stands atop the hill. This obelisk is visible from, and is within walking distance of, the Navy Yard. Climb its 294 steps for good views.

USS *Constitution* The highlight of the Yard is "Old Ironsides." Launched in Boston in 1797, she is still part of the US Navy, whose sailors lead tours round the cramped quarters. Vulnerable though the wooden sides seem now, it was her tough live-oak frames that enabled her to survive the War of 1812 undefeated and win her nickname. After surviving three wars, the vessel was frail and needed to be heavily reconstructed. She takes a turn in Boston Harbor every July 4, so that the side that faces the elements can be changed.

More to See

AMES AND SEARS BUILDINGS
The 14-floor, 1889 Ames Building dominated the skyline until the Custom House Tower was built.
🚇 K5 ✉ 1 Court Street 🚉 State

CHARLES RIVER BOAT TOURS
http://charlesriverboat.com
A leisurely cruise among the sailboats and crew teams on the Charles River offers a new perspective on the city, with views of Beacon Hill, the Boston skyline, the Esplanade and the Harvard residential houses. A 10am tour explores the locks and harbor.
🚇 H3 ✉ 100 CambridgeSide Place, Suite 320, Cambridge ☎ 617/621-3001
🕐 Hours vary by season; call for details 🚉 Lechmere 💰 Expensive ❓ Main docking location at Canal Park, CambridgeSide Galleria, Cambridge

CHRISTOPHER COLUMBUS WATERFRONT PARK
This is a small waterfront park near Faneuil Hall Marketplace and North End. Sit under the trellis or on the grass with a picnic and watch the boats.
🚇 L4 ✉ Atlantic Avenue 🚉 Aquarium
🕐 Daily 💰 Free

CUSTOM HOUSE TOWER
The 30-floor clock tower (1915) is a Boston landmark and was for a long time the city's tallest building. At street level you see how odd it looks stuck on the roof of the original Custom House, built in 1847 in Greek Revival style, at what was then the water's edge. It is now a hotel, but the public can go up to the observatory for great views.
🚇 K5 ✉ 3 McKinley Square
🕐 Observatory: Sat–Thu at 2pm 🚉 State, Aquarium 💰 Donation to charity

JAMES CURLEY STATUES
A colorful Boston Irish mayor, James Curley (1874–1958) comes both seated and standing (Lloyd Lillie, 1980) at Faneuil Hall.
🚇 K4 ✉ North/Union streets 🚉 State

MUSEUM OF AFRO-AMERICAN HISTORY
www.afroammuseum.org
A museum dedicated to the history

The Custom House Tower at night

Commercial Wharf adjacent to Christopher Columbus Park on the waterfront

of African-Americans in Boston is housed in the African Meeting House, built in 1806 and the oldest surviving African-American church building in the US. Once a center for social and political activity, it is now a focal point on the Black Heritage Trail, a 1.6-mile (2.5km) guided or self-guided walking tour of pre-Civil War Beacon Hill sites, including the Abiel Smith School and the Robert Gould Shaw Monument.

➕ J5 ✉ 46 Joy Street ☎ 617/725-0022 🕐 Memorial Day–Labor Day Mon–Sat 10–4 🚇 Charles/MGH, Park Street, Government Center 💷 Donation

NEW ENGLAND HOLOCAUST MEMORIAL
www.nehm.org
Six tall glass towers, the work of Stanley Saitowitz (1995), recall Nazi death camps. Etched numerals represent the Holocaust's six million victims. The memorial is especially poignant after dark, when it is floodlighted.

➕ K4 ✉ Union Street 🕐 Daily 🚇 State

NICHOLS HOUSE MUSEUM
www.nicholshousemuseum.org
One of Boston's earliest Federal-style houses, this elegant four-floor Beacon Hill house was built by Charles Bulfinch in 1804 and is furnished with Nichols family art and antiques.

➕ J5 ✉ 55 Mount Vernon Street ☎ 617/227-6993 🕐 Apr–Oct Tue–Sat 11–4; Nov–Mar Thu–Sat 11–4. By tour only; last tour starts at 4pm 🚇 Park Street 💷 Moderate

SAMUEL ADAMS STATUE
Anne Whitney's (1880) portrayal of the defiant revolutionary leader, in front of Faneuil Hall.

➕ K5 ✉ Congress Street 🚇 State

TD GARDEN
www.tdbanknorthgarden.com
The old West End is not an exciting district, but has the TD Garden, home to the Celtics and Bruins, next to North Station.

➕ J3 ✉ 150 Causeway Street ☎ Ticketmaster: 800/745-3000 🚇 North Station

Statue of Paul Revere in front of the Old North Church

The African Meeting House hosts the Museum of Afro-American History

Freedom Trail

The Freedom Trail links sites from Boston's Colonial and revolutionary era. Follow the red line on the sidewalk (pictured above).

DISTANCE: 1.5 miles (2.5km) **ALLOW:** 1–4 hours

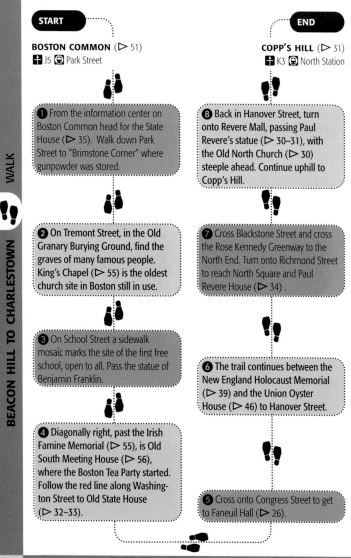

START

BOSTON COMMON (▷ 51)
🚇 J5 Ⓟ Park Street

END

COPP'S HILL (▷ 31)
🚇 K3 Ⓟ North Station

❶ From the information center on Boston Common head for the State House (▷ 35). Walk down Park Street to "Brimstone Corner" where gunpowder was stored.

❽ Back in Hanover Street, turn onto Revere Mall, passing Paul Revere's statue (▷ 30–31), with the Old North Church (▷ 30) steeple ahead. Continue uphill to Copp's Hill.

❷ On Tremont Street, in the Old Granary Burying Ground, find the graves of many famous people. King's Chapel (▷ 55) is the oldest church site in Boston still in use.

❼ Cross Blackstone Street and cross the Rose Kennedy Greenway to the North End. Turn onto Richmond Street to reach North Square and Paul Revere House (▷ 34).

❸ On School Street a sidewalk mosaic marks the site of the first free school, open to all. Pass the statue of Benjamin Franklin.

❻ The trail continues between the New England Holocaust Memorial (▷ 39) and the Union Oyster House (▷ 46) to Hanover Street.

❹ Diagonally right, past the Irish Famine Memorial (▷ 55), is Old South Meeting House (▷ 56), where the Boston Tea Party started. Follow the red line along Washington Street to Old State House (▷ 32–33).

❺ Cross onto Congress Street to get to Faneuil Hall (▷ 26).

40

Shopping

BEACON HILL CHOCOLATES

Fine chocolate is transformed into delectable and beautiful gifts, packaged in elegant boxes. The tiny shop's entrance is just around the corner from Charles Street.
H5 92B Pinckey Street
☎ 617/725-1900
Charles/MGH

BLACK INK

An eclectic selection of funky gifts and novelties: shark staplers, alphabet cookie cutters, bright green frog banks, architectural city guides.
H5 101 Charles Street
☎ 617/723-3883
Charles/MGH, Arlington

BOSTON PEWTER COMPANY

All manner of traditional, hand-crafted pewter items fill shelves here, including pieces for the home (lighting, sculpture and dishes) and gift ware (picture frames, jewelry).
K5 South Market, Faneuil Hall Marketplace
☎ 617/523-1776 State, Government Center

BOSTONIAN SOCIETY MUSEUM SHOP

Buy a little piece of New England history from this store created to support Boston's Historical Society. The group peddles books about New England's past, plus quilts, teas, mugs and prints.
K5 South Canopy,

Faneuil Hall Marketplace
☎ 617/742-4744 State, Government Center

BUILD-A-BEAR WORKSHOP

Teddy bears are the focus, although this kid-pleasing shop has plush dinosaurs and other stuffed animals, too. Everything the well-dressed bear needs is here: clothes, holiday costumes, boots, paw brushes, Santa beards, furniture, sandals and all the latest in bearwear.
K5 North Market, Faneuil Hall Marketplace
☎ 617/227-2478
Government Center/State

CAMBRIDGESIDE GALLERIA

More than 120 stores and restaurants including Borders, Sears, Macy's, Best Buy, California Pizza Kitchen and the Cheesecake Factory.
G3 100 CambridgeSide

THE CHAIN

Most of the major American clothes chains are represented in the city: Abercrombie & Fitch (Faneuil Hall Marketplace), Banana Republic (CambridgeSide Galleria, Newbury Street), French Connection, Giorgio Armani (Newbury Street), The Limited (Massachusetts Avenue), Saks Fifth Avenue, Ann Taylor and Chico's (Prudential Center).

Place ☎ 617/621-8666
Lechmere

COACH

The sleek downtown outpost of the popular and high-quality international leather goods company sells an impressive selection of the collection's handbags, business gear, shoes and other accessories. Also at Copley Place.
K5 South Market, Faneuil Hall Marketplace
☎ 617/723-1777 State, Government Center

CRATE & BARREL

Well-designed, affordable household goods: Egyptian cotton sheets, table linen, hand-blown glass, kitchen utensils. Also at 777 Boylston Street and 1045 Massachusetts Avenue.
K5 Faneuil Hall Marketplace ☎ 617/742-6025
State, Government Center

DANISH COUNTRY ANTIQUES

True to its name, this gem full of imported finds sells well-preserved, rustic pieces from Denmark. Don't miss the fine selection of tables—for the kitchen, dining room or living room.
H4 138 Charles Street
☎ 617/227-1804
Charles/MGH

EUGENE GALLERIES

Specializes in old maps and prints, with a good selection covering Boston.

This is the place to discover heirlooms and excellent gifts.
⊞ H5 ✉ 76 Charles Street
☎ 617/227-3062
Ⓒ Charles/MGH

FLAT OF THE HILL
One of the city's most charming gift boutiques, this is crammed with garden accessories, hand-knit throws, pretty stationery and more.
⊞ H5 ✉ 60 Charles Street
☎ 617/619-9977
Ⓒ Charles/MGH

FOUR PREPPY PAWS
Everything imaginable and more, for that dog or cat (or maybe its owner).
⊞ H5 ✉ 103 Charles Street
☎ 617/723-0112
Ⓒ Charles/MGH, Arlington

GEOCLASSICS
Geological wonders become fine jewelry, displayed to show their origin. For example, a necklace of quartz beads lies against a dramatic quartz crystal.
⊞ K5 ✉ 7 North Market, Faneuil Hall Marketplace
☎ 617/523-6112
Ⓒ Government Center, State

GOOD, INC
A range of simple but design-conscious gifts.
⊞ H4 ✉ 88 Charles Street
☎ 617/722-9200
Ⓒ Charles/MGH

HILTON'S TENT CITY
Good place for hiking and a range of camping equipment and

performance clothing.
⊞ K4 ✉ 272 Friend Street
☎ 617/227-9242 Ⓒ North Station

HOLIDAY BOUTIQUE
Modern, sassy women's fashions line the racks of this small but well-stocked shop. Find moderately priced designs by Frost French, Lauren Moffatt, Petit Bateau, Cynthia Vincent and denim by Rock & Republic.
⊞ H5 ✉ 53 Charles Street
☎ 617/973-9730
Ⓒ Charles/MGH

KOO DE KIR
The place to find housewares—from pitchers and calfskin rugs to transferware plates and star-shaped chandeliers—that are equal parts funky and classic. Home accessories and furniture from all over the globe.
⊞ H5 ✉ 65 Chestnut Street
☎ 617/723-8111
Ⓒ Charles/MGH

LINENS ON THE HILL
Fine French linens:

CHARLES STREET
This is a delightful street of stores and restaurants, running north from the Public Garden through the flat area of Beacon Hill. It specializes in (mostly pricey) antiques shops but has several gift shops and galleries, too, and a selection of places where you can get a bite to eat.
⊞ J4 Ⓒ Arlington, Charles

Sheets, pillowcases, tablecloths. Also nightgowns and robes.
⊞ H6 ✉ 52 Charles Street
☎ 617/227-1255
Ⓒ Charles/MGH, Arlington

MUSEUM OF FINE ARTS GIFT SHOP
Posters, prints, books, educational toys and museum reproductions of jewelry displayed in the museum collections.
⊞ K5 ✉ 3 South Market Building, Faneuil Hall Marketplace ☎ 617/720-1266
Ⓒ State, Government Center

THE RED WAGON
Bright, creatively casual T-shirt sets, dresses and more for babies and young children.
⊞ H5 ✉ 69 Charles Street
☎ 617/524-9402
Ⓒ Charles/MGH

SAVENOR'S
The late, mighty culinary queen Julia Child used to order her meats from this specialty foods market, where you'll find everything from giraffe meat to wild mushrooms.
⊞ H5 ✉ 160 Charles Street
☎ 617/723-6528
Ⓒ Charles/MGH

WISH BOUTIQUE
A friendly, colorful women's clothing store, hung with frocks by Nanette Lapore, Rebecca Taylor and Theory.
⊞ H5 ✉ 49 Charles Street
☎ 617/227-4441
Ⓒ Charles/MGH

Entertainment and Nightlife

21ST AMENDMENT

www.21stboston.com
Across from the State House, a good spot to refuel with beer and pressed sandwiches while walking the Freedom Trail. At night, it attracts a young local crowd.

➕ J5 ✉ 150 Bowdoin Street
☎ 617/227-7100
🚇 Bowdoin, Park Street

THE BLACK ROSE

www.irishconnection.com/blackrose.html
This family Irish bar is one of the best places to catch live Celtic music—and line your stomach with corned beef and Guinness.

➕ J5 ✉ 160 State Street
☎ 617/742-2286 🚇 State

CHEERS

www.cheersboston.com
After standing in line for hours, tourists are often disappointed that the inside of the Bull & Finch on Beacon Hill, which served as the model for the television show *Cheers*, looks nothing like it does on TV. Instead, go by the new Cheers bar in Faneuil Hall, which was designed to an exact replica of the set.

➕ K5 ✉ 84 Beacon Street / Faneuil Hall Marketplace
☎ 617/227-9605 or 617/227-0150
🚇 Charles/MGH, Arlington, Haymarket

HONG KONG AT FANEUIL HALL

www.hongkongboston.com
Two words: scorpion bowls! The booze-filled punch packs a wallop, and fuels a fun but cheesy dance scene.

➕ K5 ✉ 65 Chatham Street
☎ 617/227-2226 🚇 State

IMPROV ASYLUM

www.improvasylum.com
Comedy theater that features sketch and improvisational comedy at a North End cabaret-style theater. Advance tickets recommended.

➕ K4 ✉ 216 Hanover Street
☎ 617/263-6887 🕓 Shows Tue–Sun 🚇 Haymarket

LAST HURRAH

www.omnihotels.com
Black-and-white photos

Odyssey
Operates evening cruises on a 600-passenger yacht, plus a Sunday jazz brunch and weekday lunches (reservations required).

✉ Rowes Wharf
☎ 617/654-9710 or 888/741-0281;
www.odysseycruises.com

The Spirit of Boston
Has DJs and shows on its dinner-dance cruises.

✉ World Trade Center
☎ 617/748-1450;
www.spiritcruises.com
🕓 Lunch and dinner cruises daily Jun–Oct. Call for winter schedule

from Boston's Golden Age line the walls in the Parker House's upscale hotel bar. Clientele is a mix of hotel guests and City Hall politicos.

➕ K5 ✉ 60 School Street
☎ 617/227-8600
🚇 Government Center, State

THE PURPLE SHAMROCK

www.irishconnection.com/shamrock.html
By day the restaurant serves Irish and New England favorites. After dark, it's rowdy and fun with nightly entertainment that is a mix of live music, karaoke and DJs.

➕ K5 ✉ 1 Union Street
☎ 617/227-2060 🚇 State, Government Center

SILVERTONE BAR & GRILL

A stylish subterranean bar that draws a mixed crowd of students and professionals for specialty cocktails and gooey comfort food. Crowded on weekends.

➕ K5 ✉ 69 Bromfield Street
☎ 617/338-7887
🚇 Park Street

SEVENS

Often referred to as the "real Cheers," this Charles Street institution draws a slice from all walks of life to drink frosty ones at wooden booths and gripe about the Sox.

➕ H5 ✉ 77 Charles Street
☎ 617/523-9074
🚇 Charles/MGH

Restaurants

PRICES

Prices are approximate, based on a 3-course meal for one person.

$$$	over $40
$$	$20–$40
$	under $20

ANTICO FORNO ($)

Excellent Italian specialties at this casual, small spot, all whisked from the brick oven to your table. Try the fusilli with vegetables, goat cheese and basil or the swordfish with citrus and pickled onions.

🚇 K4 ✉ 93 Salem Street ☎ 617/723-6733 🕐 Lunch Mon–Sat; dinner daily 🚇 Haymarket

ARTÙ ($$)

Country-style Italian cooking and friendly staff. Try chicken layered with eggplant and mozzarella. There is a second branch at 89 Charles Street.

🚇 K4 ✉ 6 Prince Street, North End ☎ 617/742-4336 🕐 From 11am 🚇 Haymarket

BEACON HILL BISTRO ($$)

A soothing, neutral-toned bistro serving excellent seafood dishes and a creative late-night bar menu. Don't miss top-notch desserts like the rhubarb clafouti with macerated strawberries and milk-flavored ice cream.

🚇 H5 ✉ 25 Charles Street ☎ 617/723-7575 🕐 Breakfast, lunch, dinner daily 🚇 Charles/MGH

CAFFÈ VITTORIA ($)

Popular North End spot for an after-dinner coffee, pastry or *gelato*.

🚇 K4 ✉ 296 Hanover Street ☎ 617/227-7606 🕐 Daily 7am–midnight 🚇 Haymarket

CANTINA ITALIANA ($$)

A relaxed eatery serving excellent regional food.

🚇 K4 ✉ 346 Hanover Street, North End ☎ 617/723-4577 🕐 Mon–Sat from 11.30; Sun from noon 🚇 Haymarket

DURGIN PARK ($$)

www.durgin-park.com

One of the oldest dining rooms in the US. The roast beef melts in the mouth and there's hard-to-find traditional fare like Indian pudding. Crowded; very informal—but the waiters make a thing of being rude.

🚇 K5 ✉ Faneuil Hall Marketplace ☎ 617/227-2038 🕐 Mon–Sat 11.30–10, Sun

SEAFOOD OPTIONS

Nowadays some of Boston's finest fish is served outside of the traditional seafood restaurants listed on these pages. Most of the city's best eating spots do an excellent job with seafood preparations, and these dishes are taking an increasingly large share of their menus. Other good choices for fresh seafood are any of the Chinatown restaurants with live-from-the-tanks fish.

11.30–9 🚇 State, Aquarium, Government Center

LA FAMIGLIA GIORGIO'S RESTAURANT ($$)

All the favorites, in generous portions, are served at this family-friendly Roman-style restaurant. Teachers and students with ID get 20 percent discount, and the children's menu offers more choices than most.

🚇 K4 ✉ 112 Salem Street ☎ 617/367-6711 🕐 Lunch and dinner daily 🚇 Haymarket

HUNGRY I ($$$)

Tiny, intimate basement offering a small but inventive menu.

🚇 H5 ✉ 71 Charles Street ☎ 617/227-3524 🕐 Lunch Thu–Fri; dinner daily; brunch Sun 🚇 Charles/MGH

KINGFISH HALL ($$–$$$)

www.toddenglish.com

Flashy Faneuil Hall fish joint. Creative, if pricey, fish dishes in an eclectic modern (often noisy) room.

🚇 K5 ✉ 188 S. Market Street ☎ 617/523-8862 🕐 Lunch Mon–Sat; dinner daily; brunch Sun 🚇 State, Government Center

LALA ROKH ($$)

Refined Persian cuisine at this casually elegant, low-ceilinged restaurant. Specialties include exotic creations like chicken with rose petals, cumin and

cinnamon. The saffron ice cream is a must-try.

✚ H5 ✉ 97 Mount Vernon Street ☎ 617/720-5511 🕐 Lunch Mon–Fri, dinner daily 🚇 Charles/MGH

MAMMA MARIA ($$$)

www.mammamaria.com
Highly regarded elegant North End Italian, offering imaginative cooking and gracious service. Try the *osso buco* (traditional shin of veal stew).

✚ K4 ✉ 3 North Square, North End ☎ 617/523-0077 🕐 Dinner daily 🚇 Haymarket

NAPOLI PASTRY SHOP ($)

In summer the floor-to-ceiling windows of this shop open to make it a sidewalk café. The cakes and *cannoli* are made on the premises, perfect accompaniments for a steaming cappuccino; the *gelato* is excellent.

✚ K4 ✉ 120 Salem Street ☎ 617/742-0809 🕐 Daily 7am–11pm 🚇 Haymarket

NO. 9 PARK ($$$)

New American fare in a dignified if simple dining room. Chef Barbara Lynch has a way with duck; her signature crispy duck is deliciously crisp outside, meltingly tender within. Less expensive café menu.

✚ J5 ✉ 9 Park Street ☎ 617/742-9991 🕐 Lunch Mon–Fri; dinner Mon–Sat 🚇 Park Street

PLAZA III, THE KANSAS CITY STEAKHOUSE ($$)

A white-linened dining room sets the scene for civilized steakhouse dining. Lunches get particularly busy, as the neighboring Financial District employees file in.

✚ K5 ✉ 101 South Market Building, Faneuil Hall Marketplace ☎ 617/720-5570 🕐 Lunch, dinner daily 🚇 State, Government Center

PREZZA ($$$)

www.prezza.com
Modern Italian fare in a hip space. Try the home-made pastas such as pea tortelli with Virginia ham. Save room for the chocolate hazelnut cake.

✚ L4 ✉ 24 Fleet Street, North End ☎ 617/227-1577 🕐 Dinner daily 🚇 Haymarket

SLUGGER'S DUGOUT ($)

www.sluggersdugout.com
If you're dying for a good ol' burger (black angus beef) or bit of ice cream (flavors such as black

NEW ENGLAND DISHES

Try these: lobster, clam chowder, scrod, quahog (a large clam, pronounced "ko hog"), Boston baked beans (cooked long and slow in an earthenware pot), Boston cream pie (chocolate-covered and custard-filled white cake), Indian pudding (cornmeal, milk and molasses, cooked long and slow).

raspberry and bubble gum), head to Slugger's.

✚ K5 ✉ Quincy Market Building, Faneuil Hall Marketplace ☎ 617-723-3635 🕐 Lunch, dinner daily 🚇 State, Government Center

SULTAN'S KITCHEN ($)

Turkish-Middle Eastern takeout (with a few tables), convenient for lunch or early dinner; good vegetarian dishes, salads and kebabs.

✚ K5 ✉ 116 State Street, Financial District ☎ 617/570-9009 🕐 Mon–Fri 11–8; Sat 11–4.30 🚇 State

UNION OYSTER HOUSE ($$)

More regarded as an historic landmark than an eatery, Union Oyster House has been open since 1826, and has hosted everyone from John F. Kennedy to Leonardo DiCaprio.

✚ K4 ✉ 41 Union Street ☎ 617/227-2750 🕐 Lunch, dinner daily 🚇 Haymarket

UPPER CRUST PIZZERIA ($)

Uncommonly good, gourmet pizzas are created here—all thin-crusted, and all straight out of the oven. The Margherita is a favorite, but don't bypass other toppings such as baby clams, prosciutto, *asiago* and pineapple.

✚ H5 ✉ 20 Charles Street ☎ 617/723-9600 🕐 Lunch, dinner daily 🚇 Charles/MGH

The bustling area running from Boston Common and the Public Garden to the Waterfront takes you through the Theater District, Chinatown and the Financial District.

Sights	50–56	Top 25	**TOP 25**
Walk	57	Boston Athenaeum ▷ 50	
Shopping	58	Boston Common and Public Garden ▷ 51	
Entertainment and Nightlife	59–60	Institute of Contemporary Art ▷ 52	
Restaurants	61–62	New England Aquarium ▷ 53	

Boston Common to the Waterfront

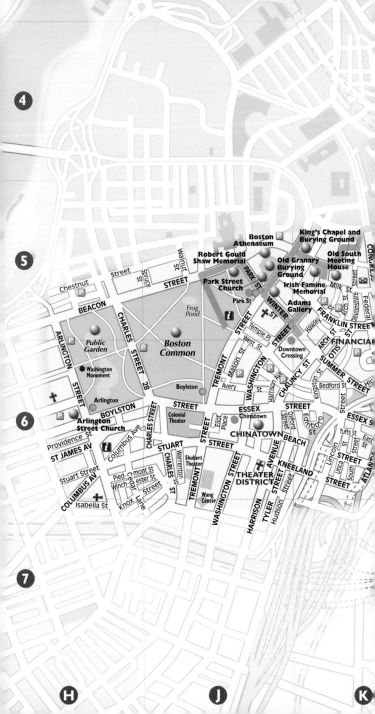

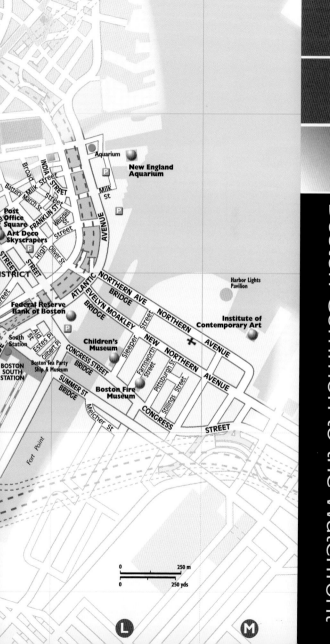

Aquarium

New England Aquarium

Broad

INDIA STREET

Street

Batten

MILK STREET

March St.

Milk Street

Milk St.

AVENUE

Wendell St.

Post Office Square

FRANKLIN ST

Street

Art Deco Skyscrapers

High

Oliver St.

STREET

STREET

ISTRICT

NORTHERN AVE

ATLANTIC

BRIDGE

Harbor Lights Pavilion

EVELYN MOAKLEY

NORTHERN

Federal Reserve Bank of Boston

BRIDGE

Institute of Contemporary Art

South Station

Estes Pl.

3rd St.

Gilbert St.

Sleeper Street

AVENUE

Children's Museum

CONGRESS STREET

NEW

NORTHERN

BOSTON SOUTH STATION

Boston Tea Party Ship & Museum

BRIDGE

Farnsworth Street

Pittsburgh St.

Stillings Street

SUMMER ST

Boston Fire Museum

BRIDGE

Melcher St.

CONGRESS

STREET

AVENUE

Fort Point

| 0 | | 250 m |
| 0 | | 250 yds |

Ⓛ   Ⓜ

Boston Athenaeum

TOP 25

Take a guided tour of the Boston Athenaeum Library

THE BASICS

www.bostonathenaeum.org

⊞ J5

✉ 10 1/2 Beacon Street

☎ 617/227-0270

🕐 First floor: Mon, Wed 8.30–8, Tue, Thu, Fri 9–5.30; also Sep–May Sat 9–4. Other floors: by tour only, Tue, Thu 3pm (you must reserve ahead)

🍴 Nearby

Ⓟ Park Street

♿ Wheelchair access

✋ Free

❓ Lectures, concerts

HIGHLIGHTS

● The civilized, unhurried atmosphere
● The reading rooms
● Paintings and sculptures
● Views of Old Granary Burying Ground

TIP

● Stop by the Athenaeum on Tuesday or Thursday at 3pm for a docent tour of all five floors of the library. Call ahead to reserve a space.

Many Bostonians have never been here. You must see what they are missing. Leave 21st-century hassle behind and enter what Henry James called "the haunt of all the most civilized."

Temple of culture When the Athenaeum library moved to 10 1/2 Beacon Street in 1849 it had been the center of intellectual and cultural life in Boston for more than 40 years. Indeed, the paintings and sculptures it had accumulated formed the core of the Museum of Fine Arts' original collection. Founded in 1807 to foster scholarship, literature, science and the visual arts, it remains the haunt of Boston's intellectual elite. Extensions and refurbishment have restored the building to its former glory and brought its facilities into the 21st century. The collection of 600,000 volumes has books from George Washington's personal library.

Silence Visitors have access to the first floor at any time and to other floors by guided tour. Many of the library's important paintings hang in a large first-floor gallery. Glass walls screen a newspaper and magazine reading room. A splendid old elevator (complemented by a modern one) takes members up to the second-floor reading room and print room, a third-floor room where members browse and converse, and a silent fifth-floor research room. On all floors long windows overlook the Old Granary Burying Ground, leather-upholstered chairs are drawn up to antique tables, oriental rugs cover the floors, books line the walls, busts and statues stand on plinths.

Pedal-powered Swan Boats, which date from 1877, transport visitors across the pond

Boston Common and Public Garden

Very different in history and character, these adjoining pieces of public open space, separated by Charles Street, right in the heart of the city, are held in deep affection. Without them, Boston just wouldn't be Boston.

Boston Common The oldest public park in the US owes its origins to early British settlers who in 1634 acquired the land from a Reverend William Blaxton for common grazing. It was also where criminals were hanged, witches were dunked and the dead were buried (in the Central Burying Ground, by Boylston Street). Here, British soldiers camped and George Washington addressed the crowds after Independence. Early in the 1800s paths were laid out and fountains and monuments erected. It is still a place for speeches and demonstrations, but also for street performers and concerts or, in winter, ice-skating at Frog Pond. Safe by day, it's best avoided at night.

The Public Garden Much more genteel and decorative, this was created as a botanical garden in 1837. Hundreds of trees were planted and beds, lawns and a lacing of footpaths were laid out. The garden is perennially beautiful and often fairy-tale-like. The focal point is a pond, with a pretty little cast-iron suspension bridge (the world's smallest). Here, in summer, you can ride the famous Swan Boats. Sculptures include a striking equestrian George Washington (Thomas Ball, 1869) and the Ether Monument, marking the first use of ether as an anaesthetic, here in Boston, in 1846.

THE BASICS

✚ J5/H5

✉ Bounded by Beacon, Park, Tremont, Boylston, Arlington streets

☎ Swan Boats: 617/ 522-1966. Ice-skating: 617/635-2120

🕐 Public Garden: daily dawn–10pm. Swan Boats: Apr–Sep. Ice-skating: Dec–Mar

🍴 Nearby

🚇 Park Street, Boylston, Arlington

♿ Garden and Common free. Swan Boats, skating inexpensive

TIPS

● The Common's Parkman Bandstand frequently features free concerts.

● Try to avoid bringing a car into Central Boston, but if you must, beneath Boston Common is one of the most affordable garages downtown (enter from Charles Street).

Institute of Contemporary Art

The superb new home of the Institute (left); The Founders' Gallery (right)

THE BASICS

www.icaboston.org

🚇 M6

✉ 100 Northern Avenue

☎ 617/478-3100, Box Office 617/478-3103

🕐 Tue–Wed, Sat–Sun 10–5, Thu–Fri 10–9

🍴 Café open same hours

Ⓜ Courthouse

♿ Wheelchair access

💲 Expensive (free Thu 5–9pm and for families the last Sat of each month, excluding Dec)

❓ Performances, concerts

HIGHLIGHTS

● The architecture
● The interpretation of exhibits
● The outstanding gift shop

TIP

● While in the neighborhood, enjoy lunch or dinner at Aura, a few steps down Northern Avenue in the Seaport Hotel.

Until the opening of this stunning building in December 2006, there was little reason for visitors to cross the Fort Point Channel into South Boston's waterfront district. Now there are several: the structure itself, the collection and HarborWalk.

The building The first US work of the architectural firm of Diller Scofidio + Renfro, the dramatic building reaches out over the harbor with a breathtaking cantilevered facade. Its expanses of glass overlook superb views, and the area sheltered by the overhang creates an amphitheater for performances with the water as a backdrop.

The art Superb though the views may be, the building also offers extraordinary opportunities for displaying contemporary art and mounting multimedia presentations. The Institute's permanent collection of 21st-century art includes works by leading names, among them Philip-Lorca diCorcia, Mona Hatoum, Ambreen Butt, Paul Chan, Rineke Dijkstra and Thomas Hirschorn. As the museum's holdings continue to grow, the main emphasis is on the well-interpreted special exhibitions that explore the complex nature of artistic expression.

HarborWalk Part of a planned 47-mile (76km) promenade that will cover Boston's entire waterfront, the section of HarborWalk that connects Rowe's Wharf to the Institute is worth walking for its own art. In addition to the harbor views, the walkway is lined with beautiful iron sculptures representing marine themes.

A replica coral reef home to tropical fish (left); the modern aquarium building (right)

New England Aquarium

One of the largest aquatic collections in the world, this is a popular family excursion. A spiral ramp leads you around a vast cylindrical tank swirling with sea creatures of every imaginable size, shape and hue.

Penguins, sharks and electric eels In the penguin pool at the base of the Giant Ocean Tank pick out the world's smallest species, the Little Blues, then head left, past the Medical Center. Either go outside for a sea-lion presentation or turn right, up the straight ramp, to the Thinking Gallery, where you can compare your hearing to that of a dolphin and your skeleton to that of a fish. The Freshwater Gallery has above- and below-surface views of a flooded Amazon forest complete with anaconda, alongside, by contrast, a New England trout stream. Don't miss the electric eel. Eventually, you reach the top of the huge tank at the heart of the Aquarium. At feeding times, approximately hourly, staff dive in, scattering squid for the bigger fish, jamming lettuce into the fiberglass coral reef for the angel fish, hand-feeding the sharks and giving the turtles their vitamin-enriched gelatin (to keep their shells hard). Notice how all the fish swim in the same direction, into the current set up by the filter, to get more oxygen.

From big screen to deep waters To experience places that cannot be re-created in the aquarium, watch one of the aquatic films showing at the IMAX theater. Alternatively, take the excellent Voyager III whale-watching trip.

THE BASICS

www.neaq.org

🔢 L5

✉ Central Wharf

☎ 617/973-5200

🕐 Jul 1–Labor Day Mon–Thu 9–6, Fri–Sun, holidays 9–7; rest of year Mon–Fri 9–5, Sat, Sun, holidays 9–6

🍴 On premises

♿ Aquarium & Good

✋ Expensive (IMAX is extra). Boston CityPass applies

❓ Concerts, lectures, tours, shop, whale-watching Apr–Oct ☎ 617/973-5200

HIGHLIGHTS

● Giant Ocean Tank
● Medical Center
● The huge green sea turtle
● Little Blue penguins
● Whale-watching trip
● IMAX 3D films

TIPS

● Book two weeks in advance for a special "behind the scenes" family tour ($14 per person).
● Check the daily schedule for training sessions, feeding times and shows.

More to See

ADAMS GALLERY

The history and culture of Boston and New England provides plenty of themes for collections and exhibits in this storefront gallery opposite Park Street Church (▷ 56). Everything from the Red Sox to home milk delivery have been featured in this interesting stop along the Freedom Trail.

✚ J5 ⊠ Suffolk University Law School, 120 Tremont Street ☎ 617/305-1782 🕐 Daily 9–7 🚇 Park Street

ARLINGTON STREET CHURCH

If the church is closed, ask the staff in the office (at the back) if it can be opened up. It has the largest collection of Tiffany windows in any one church.

✚ H6 ⊠ Boylston Street at Arlington Street. Office: 351 Boylston Street 🕐 Office: Mon–Fri 9–4 🚇 Arlington

ART DECO SKYSCRAPERS

There are four landmark art deco buildings in and around Post Office Square. On the corner of Water and Congress, note the elaborate facade of the John W. McCormack Post Office and Court House (1931). In Federal Street (at Franklin), the old State Street Bank, 70–75, has an external metalwork frieze and splendid metalwork in the lobby at 75–101. At 160 Federal, the United Shoe Machinery Building (1929) has exciting metalwork inside and out. Also, look for No. 60 Battery March Street, now Hilton Financial District (1928).

✚ K5 🚇 State, Downtown Crossing, Aquarium

BOSTON FIRE MUSEUM

Housed in the old firehouse on Congress Street, the museum displays shiny antique fire engines dating back to 1793, a variety of fire alarms and fire-fighting memorabilia from Boston's fires, including the great fire of 1872 and the 1942 Cocoanut Grove disaster.

✚ L6 ⊠ 344 Congress Street ☎ 617/338-9700 🕐 Sat 11–4 🚇 South Station 🖐 Donation

CHILDREN'S MUSEUM

This museum is heaven on earth for the under-10s. Try the balance climb,

Colorful neon lights inside the Children's Museum

play at shops with life-size products, squirt water jets at model boats, stretch a gigantic bubble or just enjoy the play space. And when you're all exhausted, retreat to the peace and quiet of the Japanese house.

➕ L6 ✉ 308 Congress Street, Museum Wharf ☎ 617/426-6500 ⏰ Daily 10–5 (Fri until 9) 🍴 Several nearby 🚇 South Station 💰 Moderate (Fri 5–9 $1)

CHINATOWN

Although small, the blocks between Essex Street and Kneeland Street are so intensely Asian that it's hard to believe it's still downtown Boston. The third largest Chinese community in the United States keeps the grocery stores, markets and bakeries thriving, and visitors join them to keep its many restaurants humming.

➕ J6 🚇 Chinatown, South Station

FEDERAL RESERVE BANK OF BOSTON

www.bos.frb.org

The bank hosts free concerts most Thursdays, March to June and September to December.

➕ L6 ✉ 600 Atlantic Avenue, opposite South Station ☎ 617/973-3000 ⏰ Concerts at 12.30 🚇 South Station

IRISH FAMINE MEMORIAL

These 1998 bronzes commemorate those forced by the 1840s Potato Famine to leave their native Ireland.

➕ K5 ✉ Washington/School streets

KING'S CHAPEL AND BURYING GROUND

This was built as an Anglican church in 1687 on the orders of King James II, to the indignation of the Puritan colonists. In the town's earliest (1630) burial ground lie two *Mayflower* passengers and John Winthrop, first governor of Massachusetts.

➕ K5 ✉ Tremont/School streets ☎ 617/ 227-2155 ⏰ Hours vary–call ahead. No tourists during services 🚇 Park Street

OLD GRANARY BURYING GROUND

If you see only one burial ground, make it this one. Dating from 1660,

King's Chapel later became the city's first Unitarian Church

it's the leafy resting place of many of Boston's big names—Samuel Adams, Paul Revere, James Otis, John Hancock, Peter Faneuil. Throughout, informative sign boards add historic information about the carved headstones, the people buried here and events that shaped early Boston. Many of these help to bring the place and the Colonial era to life.

➕ J5 ✉ 88 Tremont Street 🚇 Park Street

OLD SOUTH MEETING HOUSE

Starting life in 1729 as a Puritan meeting house, it was the site of the meeting that started the Boston Tea Party in 1773. Visual and audio exhibits.

➕ K5 ✉ 310 Washington Street ☎ 617/482-6439 🕐 Apr–Oct daily 9.30–5; Nov–Mar daily 10–4 🚇 State, Downtown Crossing 💷 Moderate

PARK STREET CHURCH

Notable as much for its tall white steeple as for William Lloyd Garrison's first anti-slavery speech made here in 1829. "America the Beautiful" was first sung in public here in 1831. An excellent stop for architecture lovers.

➕ J5 ✉ 1 Park Street 🕐 Jul–Aug Tue–Sat 9.30–3.30 🚇 Park Street 💷 Free

POST OFFICE SQUARE

A charming oasis, with a small café, surrounded by the Downtown area's skyscrapers. It's often filled with office workers come lunchtime, however; arrive in late morning or late afternoon to get a park bench and best appreciate the sights and sounds.

➕ K5 ✉ Between Milk and Franklin streets 🚇 State

ROBERT GOULD SHAW MEMORIAL

A sensitive bronze battle frieze by Augustus Saint-Gaudens built in 1897 in honor of the Massachusetts 54th Regiment. Shaw, depicted in the film *Glory*, led the Union's first black regiment in the Civil War. Here, for the first time, blacks were portrayed by a white artist as individuals.

➕ J5 ✉ Beacon Street, facing State House 🚇 Park Street 💷 Free

Old South Meeting House

Pausing for a rest at the base of the Robert Gould Shaw Monument

Walk This Way

The areas around Boston Common and the Waterfront are some of the most pedestrian-friendly, with historic stops and shopping.

DISTANCE: 0.8 miles (1.2km) **ALLOW:** 2–4 hours

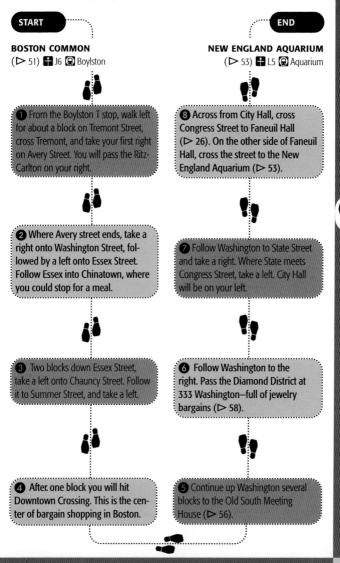

START

BOSTON COMMON
(▷ 51) ✚ J6 Ⓜ Boylston

1 From the Boylston T stop, walk left for about a block on Tremont Street, cross Tremont, and take your first right on Avery Street. You will pass the Ritz-Carlton on your right.

2 Where Avery street ends, take a right onto Washington Street, followed by a left onto Essex Street. Follow Essex into Chinatown, where you could stop for a meal.

3 Two blocks down Essex Street, take a left onto Chauncy Street. Follow it to Summer Street, and take a left.

4 After one block you will hit Downtown Crossing. This is the center of bargain shopping in Boston.

END

NEW ENGLAND AQUARIUM
(▷ 53) ✚ L5 Ⓜ Aquarium

8 Across from City Hall, cross Congress Street to Faneuil Hall (▷ 26). On the other side of Faneuil Hall, cross the street to the New England Aquarium (▷ 53).

7 Follow Washington to State Street and take a right. Where State meets Congress Street, take a left. City Hall will be on your left.

6 Follow Washington to the right. Pass the Diamond District at 333 Washington—full of jewelry bargains (▷ 58).

5 Continue up Washington several blocks to the Old South Meeting House (▷ 56).

Shopping

BRATTLE BOOKSHOP
A treasure trove of rare and secondhand books with a good section on Boston and New England. This family-owned and -run shop has been in business since the 19th century. So count on finding plenty of out-of-print and rare works, plus academic works, maps and old leather-bound books.
🚹 J5 ✉ 9 West Street
☎ 617/542-0210
🚇 Park Street

BROMFIELD PEN SHOP
Pens, from vintage early 1900s models to new Montblanc, Cross and cheap disposables.
🚹 J5 ✉ 5 Bromfield Street
☎ 617/482-9053
🚇 Park Street

DOWNTOWN CROSSING
Stores selling street fashion, shoes, jewelry, cameras and the like, plus the city's main department stores. Encompassing part of Washington, Winter and Bromfield streets, Downtown Crossing is mainly pedestrians-only.
🚹 J6 🚇 Downtown Crossing

FOOT PATHS
Elegant, casual and athletic shoes for men and women, plus a full range of hiking boots.
🚹 K6 ✉ 489 Washington Street ☎ 617/338-6008
🚇 Downtown Crossing

THE ICA STORE
Arguably the most exciting design gift shop in Boston, the ICA Store carries a stunning selection of jewelry, household decor items, children's toys, accessories and books on contemporary art and design.
🚹 L6 ✉ 100 Northern Avenue ☎ 617/478-3104
🕐 Tue–Wed, Sat–Sun 10–5, Thu–Fri 10–9 🚇 Courthouse

LOUIS BOSTON
High-quality, expensive and cutting-edge clothing for men and women in a spacious old mansion just off Newbury Street. Additionally, find international housewares, a small bookstore, plenty of accessories, a bridal registry, a hair salon and a DJ spinning station. There is also a lovely restaurant on the premises (Thu–Sat dinner)—all of which adds up to one of Boston's most fashionable addresses.
🚹 H6 ✉ 234 Berkeley Street
☎ 617/262-6100
🚇 Arlington

ST. JOHN BOUTIQUE
St. John was founded in 1962 by Robert and Marie Gray and now has stores all over the globe. Elegant, couture knitwear for women.
🚹 H6 ✉ 292 Boylston Street
☎ 617/338-6130
🚇 Arlington

SKECHERS
Very cool men's, women's and kids' athletic shoes, boots, sneakers and sandals.
🚹 J5 ✉ 417 Washington Street ☎ 617/423-0412
🚇 Downtown Crossing

TANNERY
With a staff dedicated to finding the perfect fit for each and every customer's foot, this is the place to pick up both rugged outdoor shoes and casual numbers alike. Wide range of hiking boots and sneakers (Vans, Timberland, Sebago, Rockport). Also in Brattle Street, Harvard Square.
🚹 H6 ✉ 400 Boylston Street
☎ 617/267-0899
🚇 Arlington

DOWNTOWN BARGAINS
Downtown Crossing, and all around Washington Street, is known as prime bargain territory for the marked-down jewelry sold at the **Diamond District** (at 333 Washington Street). Other discounts nearby: designer men's and women's shoes at DSW Shoe (385 Washington Street), outdoor gear at Eddie Bauer Outlet (500 Washington Street).

Entertainment and Nightlife

AQUA
www.aquaboston.com
A watering hole for young professionals draws a hip crowd for mood lighting, martinis and DJs on weekends.
🚩 K5 ✉ 120 Water Street
☎ 617/720-4900 🚇 State

BOSTON OPERA HOUSE
www.bostonoperahouse.com
Originally a vaudeville theater, this grand show-room was beautifully restored in 2004. It now features the biggest Broadway touring productions, as well as the Boston Ballet's annual performances of *The Nutcracker*.
🚩 K6 ✉ 539 Washington Street ☎ 617/259-3400
🚇 Chinatown, Boylston

CHARLES PLAYHOUSE
Shear Madness, a comedy whodunnit set in a hairdresser's, has played here since 1980. *Blue Man Group*, another long-running show, presents its offbeat mix of theater, music and performance art on the Charles' other stage.
🚩 J6 ✉ 74 Warrenton Street
☎ 617/426-5225 *(Shear Madness)*; 617/426-6912 *(Blue Man Group)* 🚇 Boylston

COLONIAL THEATRE
This lush, beautifully restored, turn-of-the-19th-century theater stages pre-Broadway productions as well as a range of other performing arts events.
🚩 J6 ✉ 106 Boylston Street
☎ 617/426-9366
🚇 Boylston

CUTLER MAJESTIC THEATRE
www.maj.org
Visiting dance troupes, world music performers, Shakespearean actors and Emerson College student productions all use the stage at this 1903 venue.
🚩 J6 ✉ 219 Tremont Street
☎ 617/824-8000
🚇 Boylston

DICK DOHERTY'S COMEDY VAULT
www.dickdoherty.com
A leading comedy club, in a former bank vault.
🚩 J6 ✉ 124 Boylston Street
☎ 800/401-2221
🕐 Shows daily 🚇 Boylston

TICKETS
BosTix sell half-price theater tickets on the day of the show (from 11am). As a fully fledged Ticketmaster outlet, it also sells full-price tickets in advance for venues in Boston and the rest of New England. Booths are at: ✉ Faneuil Hall Marketplace 🕐 Tue–Sat 10–6, Sun 11–4; ✉ Copley Square 🕐 Mon–Sat 10–6, Sun 11–4.
Tickets cover theater, concerts, museums, sports events and trolley tours. All are sold for cash only.

EMMANUEL CHURCH
www.emmanuelmusic.org
A Bach cantata every Sunday (September through May).
🚩 H6 ✉ 15 Newbury Street
☎ 617/536-3356
🚇 Arlington

FELT
www.feltboston.com
A pool hall-cum-dance club in the heart of Downtown, this multi-level nightspot features swanky decor, well-dressed patrons and regular appearances by local VIPs.
🚩 K6 ✉ 533 Washington Street ☎ 617/350-5555
🚇 Downtown Crossing

THE GOOD LIFE
www.goodlifebar.com
A stylish lounge offers a menu of gourmet pizzas and small plates for sharing. More than 125 varieties of vodka at the frozen vodka bar.
🚩 K6 ✉ 28 Kingston Street
☎ 617/451-2622
🚇 Chinatown

GYPSY BAR
www.gypsybarboston.com
Sultry interior, an intimate dance floor and events such as lingerie fashion shows combine for the city's sexiest pick-up scene.
🚩 J6 ✉ 116 Boylston Street
☎ 617/482-7799
🚇 Boylston

INSTITUTE OF CONTEMPORARY ART (ICA)

www.icaboston.org
An exhibition, film and performance space (▷ 52).
➕ M6 ✉ 100 Northern Avenue 🚇 Courthouse

JACQUE'S CABARET

And now for something completely different… Female impersonators and other offbeat performances draw everyone from drag queens to bachelorette parties.
➕ J6 ✉ 79 Broadway
☎ 617/426-8902
🚇 Arlington

JER-NE BAR

Picture windows line the walls of Ritz-Carlton's lavish hotel bar, the better for passersby to see you sipping a high-priced martini with the beautiful people.
➕ J6 ✉ 10 Avery Street
☎ 617/574-7100 🚇 Boylston

NICK'S COMEDY STOP

www.nickscomedystop.com
A well-loved Theater District comedy club with local stars and would-be stars on stage.
➕ J6 ✉ 100 Warrenton Street ☎ 617/423-2900
🕐 Shows generally Thu 8.30, Fri, Sat 8.45 🚇 Boylston

OM BAR

Tucked in a former bank vault beneath Mantra restaurant, this bar's techno music and plush decor are as chilled as its martinis.
➕ J5 ✉ 52 Temple Plaza
☎ 617/542-8111 🕐 Fri–Sat 11pm–2am 🚇 Park Street, Downtown Crossing

ROWES WHARF BAR AT BOSTON HARBOR HOTEL

www.bhh.com
Sophisticated and comfortable, Rowes Wharf Bar serves classic Boston pub fare, fine blended and single-malt scotch and serious martinis.
➕ L5 ✉ 70 Rowes Wharf
☎ 617/440-5671
🚇 Aquarium

THE ROXY

www.roxyboston.com
Favored by international students, this dance club fills a beautifully converted former ballroom. Friday is club night, Saturday Latin night.

CHEAP THEATER

Prices for productions in the Theater District can be expensive. If you are willing to roll the dice, many college theater groups offer fine productions at lower prices. For example, the **Playwright's Theatre** at Boston University (949 Commonwealth Avenue, 617/358-7529) showcases plays written or produced by students or alumni. Particularly popular is the annual **Boston Theater Marathon**, which features 50 10-minute plays every spring.

➕ J6 ✉ 279 Tremont Street
☎ 617/338-7699
🚇 Boylston, Chinatown

SILVERTONE BAR & GRILL

Popular subterranean joint just off the Common features comfy booths, creative martinis and a bar menu of comfort food like mac 'n' cheese and meatloaf. Crowded on weekends.
➕ K5 ✉ 69 Bromfield Street
☎ 617/338-7887
🚇 Park Street

THE WANG THEATRE

www.citicenter.org
A 1920s movie palace used for concerts, opera, dance and the impressive Boston Ballet (tel 617/695-6950), which performs classical and contemporary dance. The 3,600-seat theater has undergone a renovation.
➕ J6 ✉ 270 Tremont Street
☎ 617/482-9393
🚇 Boylston

THE WILBUR THEATRE AND COMEDY CONNECTION

www.thewilburtheatre.com
This first-class comedy club brings the top names in comedy to the Wilbur Theatre following its 2008 relocation from Quincy Market. There are also musical performances. Tickets available through Ticketmaster.
➕ J6 ✉ 246 Tremont Street
☎ Info: 617/248-9700. Tickets: 800/982-2787 🚇 Boylston

Restaurants

PRICES

Prices are approximate, based on a 3-course meal for one person.

$$$	over $40
$$	$20–$40
$	under $20

AURA ($$$)

www.seaportboston.com
Beautiful presentations that spotlight the inventive combinations of ingredients are the signature of Aura's imaginative chef. And the hotel's no-tipping policy applies here, too, making the prices less onerous than other restaurants of its high caliber. Desserts are outstanding.

L6 ⊠ Seaport Hotel, 1 Seaport Lane (Northern Avenue) ☎ 617/385-4300 ⊙ Dinner daily ⊜ World Trade Center

BARKING CRAB ($)

A rough-and-ready clam shack where you can eat indoors or alfresco, with downtown views across the water. Expect crowds, a wait, noise and fun.

L6 ⊠ 88 Sleeper Street, off Northern Avenue, Waterfront ☎ 617/426-2722 ⊙ From 11.30am ⊜ South Station

BISTRO DU MIDI ($$)

French Provincial cuisine in an exceptional location overlooking the Public Garden with a street-level bar serving food and drink. There is also an upstairs Garden-view French-styled dining room with wooden beams and fireplace, as well as an outdoor patio.

H6 ⊠ 227 Boylston Street, Theater District ☎ 617/426-7878 ⊙ Lunch Mon–Fri; dinner daily ⊜ Arlington

THE BRISTOL LOUNGE ($$$)

www.fourseasons.com/boston/dining
Overlooking the Public Garden and known as much for the service as the food, this is one of Boston's best formal restaurants. Upscale comfort food, including the Bristol Burger, homemade pasta and fresh seafood. Live jazz every evening.

J6 ⊠ Four Seasons Hotel (▷ 112), 200 Boylston Street ☎ 617/351-2037

PEOPLE-WATCHING

Some of the best restaurants are also the sites of its best people-watching scenes. On Boston Common, eateries like Bistro du Midi and Via Matta invite you to survey the weekend strolls taken by crowds in the verdant Public Garden. In the South End, colorful hordes of people walk the sidewalks outside bistros like Hamersley's and Union Bar & Grille. But for the most eclectic sightings, go to Newbury Street, where the outdoor cafés are perfectly perched.

⊙ Breakfast, lunch, dinner daily ⊜ Arlington

CAFÉ FLEURI ($$)

Bright and open, with well-spaced tables, this smart atrium café specializes in dishes created to showcase seasonal local ingredients. The Saturday Chocolate Bar is a decadent buffet of chocolate desserts.

K5 ⊠ The Langham Boston, 250 Franklin Street ☎ 617/956-8751 ⊙ Breakfast and lunch daily ⊜ Downtown Crossing

CHAU CHOW CITY ($$)

Traditional dim sum midday meals are a favorite here. The appetizer-size dishes are served from carts loaded with steaming buns filled with pork or bean paste, dumplings with meat, shrimp or vegetables and a variety of sweets. Every day has something different, with weekends featuring the largest selection.

J6 ⊠ 83 Essex Street ☎ 617/338-8158 ⊙ Lunch, dinner daily ⊜ Chinatown

GRILL 23 & BAR ($$$)

www.grill23.com
Steaks, prime rib of beef, lamb chops, swordfish and more. Attentive service in a men's club-style room.

H6 ⊠ 161 Berkeley Street (at Stuart Street) ☎ 617/542-2255 ⊙ Dinner daily ⊜ Arlington

LEGAL TEST KITCHEN ($$)

A modern and daring off-shoot of the Legal Sea Foods chain, this outpost serves up crunchy, corn-meal-fried clams and spicy Asian lobster. Ask to borrow one of the iPod docks on offer and you can have your own personal jukebox at your table.

⊞ L6 ⊠ 225 Northern Avenue ☎ 617/330-7430 ⚫ Lunch, dinner daily (till late) 🚇 South Station

MERITAGE ($$$)

www.meritagetherestaurant.com

A feast for the eyes as well as the palate, dining at Meritage combines a quartet of superlatives: cuisine, wine pairings, service and harbor view.

⊞ L5 ⊠ 70 Rowes Wharf ☎ 617/439-3995 ⚫ Dinner daily, breakfast Sun 🚇 Aquarium

NEW JUMBO SEAFOOD ($)

www.newjumboseafoodrestaurant.com

Crowds flock to this enclave of superlative Chinese food for the superfresh, water tank-straight-to-wok shrimp, lobster and flounder dishes. Try giant clams in black-bean sauce.

⊞ J6 ⊠ 7 Hudson Street ☎ 617/542-2823 ⚫ Lunch, dinner daily 🚇 Chinatown

NEW SHANGHAI ($)

www.newshanghaiboston.com

Upscale Chinatown eatery, specializing in Shanghai-style cuisine. Cold appetizers such as eggplant with garlic sauce.

⊞ J6 ⊠ 21 Hudson Street ☎ 617/338-6688 ⚫ Lunch, dinner daily 🚇 Chinatown

RADIUS ($$$)

www.radiusrestaurant.com

Culinary hot spot set in a 1920s one-time bank. Chef Michael Schlow serves modern French cuisine: roasted halibut with cauliflower puree and lentils, venison in green peppercorn sauce.

⊞ K6 ⊠ 8 High Street, Financial District ☎ 617/426-1234 ⚫ Lunch Mon–Fri, dinner Mon–Sat 🚇 South Station

ROWES WHARF SEA GRILLE ($$)

Boston Harbor Hotel's waterside bar-restaurant and patio is one of the town's finest casual options—for both its topnotch shrimp cocktail and its breezy, flower-festooned outdoor patio.

⊞ L5 ⊠ 70 Rowes Wharf ☎ 617/439-7000 ⚫ Breakfast, lunch, afternoon tea, dinner daily 🚇 Aquarium

SEL DE LA TERRE ($$$)

www.seldelaterre.com

Across the street from the Aquarium, this Provençal spot offers simple, delicious bistro dishes. Try not to fill up on the superb bread.

⊞ K5 ⊠ 255 State Street, Waterfront ☎ 617/720-1300 ⚫ Lunch Mon–Fri; dinner daily; brunch Sat–Sun; Wed–Sat late-night menu at the bar 🚇 South Station

TEATRO ($$–$$$)

www.teatroboston.com

A beautiful, blue-lit boite filled with theater-going crowds in for the authentic Italian menu.

⊞ J6 ⊠ 177 Tremont Street, Downtown ☎ 617/778-6841 ⚫ Dinner daily 🚇 Park Street

VIA MATTA ($$)

www.viamattarestaurant.com

Step into this chic, noisy dining room for simple but extremely fresh Italian specialties. In warm weather, make for the pretty, patio dining area.

⊞ H6 ⊠ 79 Park Plaza ☎ 617/422-0008 ⚫ Lunch Mon–Fri, dinner Mon–Sat. Closed Sun 🚇 Arlington

---

FOR VEGETARIANS

More and more restaurants include at least one entrée, and many will make up a vegetarian plate on request. In Chinatown try **Buddha's Delight** (⊠ 3 Beach Street ☎ 617/451-2395). There is sophisticated vegetarian fare Downtown. Try **Milk Street Café** (⊠ 50 Milk Street, Financial District ☎ 617/542-3663), a vegetarian-kosher luncheonette selling salads, soups and vegetable sandwiches, plus meatless entrées.

Home to some of the finest shopping and people-watching in all the city, Back Bay and the South End are also vibrant residential neighborhoods.

Sights	66–78
Walk	79
Shopping	80–81
Entertainment and Nightlife	82–83
Restaurants	84

Top 25 TOP **25**

Boston Public Library ▷ 66
Commonwealth Avenue ▷ 67
Isabella Stewart Gardner Museum ▷ 68
Museum of Fine Arts ▷ 70
Newbury Street ▷ 72
Prudential Center and Skywalk ▷ 73
The South End ▷ 74
Trinity Church and Copley Square ▷ 76

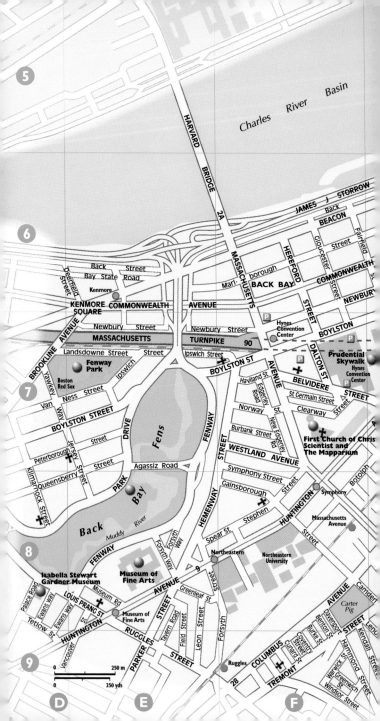

Charles River Embankment

Storrow Lagoon

MEMORIAL DRIVE 1

Street

STREET

EXETER

Commonwealth

Marlborough

Avenue

AVENUE

STREET

Newbury
Street

STREET

Prudential
Center

Harcourt St

Garrison

Prudential

prudential

Yarmouth
Street

West

Appleton
Street

Gray Street

Braddock parkway

Holyoke
Street

Durham
Street

NEWTON

AVENUE

Warren

Canton

Warren Avenue

GREENWICH
PKWY

Rutland
Square

Montgomery

CONCORD SQUARE

Pembroke

West

St

Brookline

TREMONT

COLUMBUS

Worcester

Springfield

WEST CONCORD

Rutland

Street

Street

MASSACHUSETTS

TREMONT

Street

SHAWMUT

AVENUE

Blackstone
Square

Franklin
Square

East

Street

SOUTH
END

Northampton

Street

Street

AVENUE

SHAWMUT

WASHINGTON

Ramsey
Park

G

Gibson
House
Museum

BERKELEY

Street

Street

STREET

CLARENDON STREET

2

Copley
Theater

STREET

DARTMOUTH STREET

Copley

Trinity Church
and Copley Square

Providence Street

AVENUE

JAMES

ST

Lyric
Stage

Street

Hancock
Tower

stuart

Boston
Public
Library

Back Bay/
South End

CLARENDON

BERKELEY

28

AVENUE

i

BACK BAY
STATION

COLUMBUS

CHANDLER STREET

DARTMOUTH

Lawrence St

Street

Gray Street

Avenue

STREET

Boston Center
for the Arts

STREET

Dwight Street

Milford Street

Hanson Street

Waltham

Union Pk

TREMONT

AVENUE

Bradford St

Street

STREET

DEDHAM STREET

Upton
Street

Union

Park

AVENUE

WASHINGTON

MONS
REYNOLDS
WAY

HARRISON

AVENUE

Street

MALDEN ST

Wareham Street

Plympton Street

E Canton Street

E Dedham Street

HARRISON

STREET

EAST NEWTON

St
George

St

EAST CONCORD

Worcester
Square

AVENUE

STREET

Brookline

E Canton Street

STREET

HARRISON STREET

ALBANY

H

Boston Public Library

The illuminated marble staircase (left) and cloisters (right)

This is no ordinary library. Behind its granite facade lies an opulent institution built in Renaissance palazzo style and decorated with sculptures and paintings by some of the best artists of the day.

The education of the people A people's palace dedicated to the advancement of learning was what Charles Follen McKim was commissioned to design. An architectural landmark in the classical style, facing H. H. Richardson's Romanesque Trinity Church across Copley Square, it opened its doors to the public in 1895. It is now the Research Library, the General Library being housed in the adjoining 1972 Johnson Building.

Further treasures Pass between Bela Pratt's voluptuous bronzes, *Science* and *Art* (1912), to enter through Daniel Chester French's bronze doors. Ascend the marble staircase, guarded by lions by Louis Saint-Gaudens (Augustus's brother), and from its windows catch a glimpse of the peaceful courtyard. The stairs and landing are decorated with panels by Puvis de Chavannes, whimsical representations of the muses of inspiration. The Abbey Room has paintings depicting the quest for the Holy Grail, by Edwin Austin Abbey. Bates Hall is a magnificent room; get a close-up view of its highly decorative, barrel-vaulted ceiling from the stairs that lead up to the Sargent Gallery. The John Singer Sargent murals, *Triumph of Religion*, completed in 1919, were restored in 2004. Pause to sit in the colonnaded courtyard, watching the fountain and enjoying the tranquillity.

THE BASICS

www.bpl.org
🔚 G6
✉ Copley Square
☎ 617/536-5400
🕐 Mon–Thu 9–9, Fri–Sat 9–5; Oct–May Sun 1–5
🍴 Nearby
Ⓜ Copley
♿ Good
💲 Free
❓ Tours (Dartmouth Street entrance) Mon 2.30, Tue, Thu 6, Fri–Sat 11; also Sun 2 (Oct–May only). Lectures

HIGHLIGHTS

● Puvis de Chavannes murals
● John Singer Sargent murals
● Daniel Chester French bronze doors
● The courtyard

TIP

● Free films are screened regularly in the Raab Lecture Hall.

Brownstones on Commonwealth Avenue (left and right)

Commonwealth Avenue

A Parisian-style boulevard lined with the grandest houses in Boston is at the heart of an amazing piece of 19th-century urban planning. To walk down it is to be transported to a different age.

Landfill By the 1850s, Boston was getting over-crowded. Desperate for land, developers turned to the swampy "back bay" of the Charles River, embarking on a remarkable landfill project to create a new residential district. Inspired by Paris's boulevard system, the architect Arthur Gilman planned a grid, eight blocks long and four blocks wide, with a long central mall.

Commonwealth Avenue Even the nouveau-riche industrialists who flocked to the Back Bay felt some of the Puritan restraints of the Proper Bostonians of Beacon Hill, and their rows of ostentatious brownstones are a somewhat subdued blend of Victorian styles. The centerpiece is Commonwealth Avenue. Central gardens are lined with trees; in spring magnolias bloom in profusion. The Boston Women's Memorial lies between Fairfield and Gloucester streets. Most houses are now apartments, some are offices. The châteaulike Burrage Mansion at Hereford Street stands out, with statuettes everywhere. To see inside a more average home, visit Gibson House Museum on Beacon Street.

Feeling fit? The mall is just part of a 7-mile long (11km) "Emerald Necklace" of green space stretching from Boston Common to Franklin Park.

THE BASICS

⊞ G6
🍴 Newbury and Boylston streets
🚇 Arlington, Copley, Hynes Convention Center

HIGHLIGHTS

● Magnolias in spring on Commonwealth Avenue
● Lights on the mall at Christmas
● Memorial to firemen killed in Hotel Vendome fire

TIPS

● More intimate than Commonwealth Avenue and no less beautiful is next-door Marlborough Street, which is lined with flowering dogwoods in the springtime.
● North–south streets are named alphabetically, Arlington to Hereford.

HIGHLIGHTS

● The courtyard, during any season
● The personal feel of the collection
● Afternoon concerts on many Sundays

TIPS

● In some of the rooms you must pull back curtains and open drawers to see the priceless objects that are protected from the light.
● If your first name is Isabella, congratulations—you get free admission to the museum.

The woman who created this collection of "beautiful things" had a passion for art, music and horticulture. Her finds are arranged in a Venetian-style house built around a flower-filled courtyard.

"Beautiful things" Determined to give her country "beautiful things," Mrs Gardner made a start in 1896 by buying a Rembrandt self-portrait. Her collection grew to include work by Vermeer, Giotto, Botticelli, Raphael, Degas and Matisse, as well as John Singer Sargent and James McNeill Whistler. She also bought prints and drawings, books, sculptures, ceramics and glass, tapestries, carpets, lace, stained glass, ironwork and furniture.

Music and horticulture The building itself, known as Fenway Court, and the atmosphere

El Jaleo *by John Singer Sargent in the Spanish Cloister of the Isabella Stewart Gardner Museum (left); the interior facade that overlooks the courtyard, which is filled with planting and statuary (right)*

that pervades it, is as much the creation of Mrs Gardner as her collection. She arranged her objects in a series of rooms—the Raphael Room, the Titian Room, the Gothic Room, the intimate Blue Room and more. She filled the courtyard with sculptures, plants and trees, and she celebrated the opening of her home (she lived on the top floor) to the public with a concert given by members of the Boston Symphony Orchestra. Today, concerts are held in the Tapestry Room on Sundays from September to May.

Art heist The collection suffered a terrible loss— and America's biggest art theft—in March 1990 when thieves dressed as policemen made off with 13 items, which have not been recovered. Among them were a priceless Vermeer and *The Sea of Galilee,* Rembrandt's only seascape.

THE BASICS

www.gardnermuseum.org

✚ D8

✉ 280 The Fenway

☎ 617/566-1401

🕐 Tue–Sun 11–5.
Closed Mon except most public hols

🍴 On premises

🚇 Museum of Fine Arts

♿ Good

💷 Expensive

❓ Concerts: Sep–May
Sun 1.30 ☎ 617/278-5156.
Courtyard: talks most weekdays (times posted at the information desk).
Audio tours $4. Lectures, shop

Museum of Fine Arts

HIGHLIGHTS

- Nubian collection
- Impressionist room
- Copley portraits
- Tang dynasty earthenware

TIPS

- Every first Friday night of the month there is live music and a cash bar in the Koch Gallery.
- Tickets to the museum are good for another visit within a week, so you can catch the art you missed!
- There is a free guide for families: MFA Through the Eyes of a Child.

The MFA is one of America's foremost museums. The Asian collection is unrivaled in this hemisphere, the European art is superb, the American rooms excellent. If time is limited, take a guided tour of the highlights.

Asian, Egyptian, Classical The MFA's Nubian collection is the best outside the Sudan. It is all exquisite, from the neat rows of little *shawabtis* (figurines) to the faience jewelry. The Egyptian rooms are popular, with mummies, hieroglyphics and splendid Old Kingdom sculptures. Buddhist sculptures, Chinese ceramics and Indian paintings make up part of an Asian collection.

European In the European galleries, seek out the little gem of a Rembrandt in a glass case, then

Huntington Staircase in the museum (left); Cyrus Dallin's 1909 statue Appeal to the Great Spirit *stands at the entrance to the museum (right)*

take in works of Tiepolo, Gainsborough, Turner, Delacroix, Constable and a good number of Millets. The Impressionist room is an array of familiar paintings, with works from Monet and Renoir to Gauguin. There is porcelain from all over Europe and period rooms from Britain.

American Opened in 2010, the spectacular Art of the Americas wing showcases more than 5,000 works of art from South, Central and North America. The collection includes art in all media displayed chronologically in 53 galleries, beginning with ancient Mayan ceramics through the late 20th-century art of Jackson Pollack. There are also major pieces of silver by Paul Revere, portraits by John Singleton Copley and John Singer Sargent and landscapes by Georgia O'Keeffe. Furniture and decorative arts are featured in nine period rooms.

THE BASICS

www.mfa.org

✚ E8

✉ 465 Huntington Avenue

☎ 617/267-9300

🕐 Mon–Tue 10–4.45, Wed–Fri 10–9.45, Sat–Sun 10–4.45

🍴 Choice on premises

🚇 Museum of Fine Arts

♿ Excellent

💲 Expensive. Wed 4–9.45 voluntary contribution. Boston CityPass applies

❓ Guided walks Mon–Sat. Film programs Thu–Sun. Lectures, concerts. Good shop

Newbury Street

Newbury Street houses retail and residential buildings (left and right)

THE BASICS

www.newbury-st.com

G6

Between Arlington Street and Massachusetts Avenue

Most shops open 10–6

Excellent bistros line each side of the street

Arlington, Copley, Massachusetts Avenue

Fair to excellent, depending on the business. Many have elevators

HIGHLIGHTS

● Window-shopping in Newbury Street
● People-watching in the Newbury Street cafés
● Newbury Street trompe l'oeil murals at Boston Architectural College and No. 354

Newbury Street is the place to go if you are interested in buying artwork—paintings, prints or sculpture. But art isn't the only draw at Boston's answer to Paris's Champs-Élysées.

Galleries Many a pleasant hour can be spent browsing in the galleries, stopping off in a café now and then. Individual small shops are housed in beautiful historic row houses (terraces). A concentration of galleries lies between Arlington and Fairfield streets. They display works by 19th- and 20th-century artists, in addition to contemporary pieces. The Robert Klein Gallery, at 38 Newbury Street, is the only major art gallery in New England dedicated to fine art photography. If you are interested in avant-garde galleries explore the South End, particularly around Harrison and Thayer streets.

Shop, shop, shop Shopping is also an enormous draw of the area. At the intersection with Arlington Street, where shops tend to be high-end and high-priced, shoppers find plenty of international jewelry shops, fashion designers and day spas. That stable gives way to more mid-range shops as you move toward the other end of the street, which intersects with Massachusetts Avenue. On the way there, cross mainstream fashion chains, gift shops, independent boutiques and hair salons. One thing the entire street lays claim to, however, is an abundance of cafés and restaurants. Duck into any with an outdoor patio to get a first-rate spot for people-watching.

The view from the tower at night (left); retail outlets (middle); the Prudential Tower (right)

Prudential Center and Skywalk

An architecturally unremarkable building offering bird's-eye views of Boston and the New England countryside from its 50th floor. Drop back closer to the ground for shops and eating places.

Skywalk at the Prudential Tower The Prudential Tower is architecturally undistinguished, part of the 1960s Prudential Center office and shopping complex. But take the elevator to the Skywalk on the 50th floor and you have stunning 360-degree views—weather permitting, as far as the mountains of New Hampshire. Pick out the gold dome of the State House; peer down onto the rooftops of the neat Back Bay homes and over the Charles River to MIT and Cambridge; see the parks of the "Emerald Necklace" stretching into the distance; look out to the Boston Harbor Islands. Interactive exhibits cover key historical and sporting events, as well as distinguished buildings and residents. Looking to relax while soaking up that same stunning view? The Top of the Hub restaurant, on the Pru's 52nd floor, looks out to the twinkling city and beyond; be sure to stop in for a cocktail or dessert, and a city profile you won't soon forget.

Down to earth Meanwhile, on the lower levels of the building, find plenty of indoor shopping and snacking. The food courtyard caters to diners-in-a-rush with chain cafés (some healthy, some not) and several more sedate sit-down establishments, while the stores lure shoppers in for high-end jewelry, international fashions, quality stationery and even flowers.

THE BASICS

www.prudentialcenter.com

G7

Prudential Tower, 800 Boylston Street

617/859-0648

Daily 10–10. Skywalk: Mar–Oct 10–9.30, Nov–Feb 10–8

Top of the Hub; choice in Prudential Center

Prudential, Hynes Convention Center

Excellent

Expensive. Boston CityPass applies

HIGHLIGHTS

● Views from the Pru after snow
● Views from the Pru at night
● Top of the Hub bar and restaurant on the 52nd floor
● Sushi at Haru, outside the Huntington Avenue entrance
● Crane Stationery for top-quality cards and papers

The South End

HIGHLIGHTS

● Excellent bistros and restaurants in Tremont and Washington streets
● Cutting-edge art galleries, trendy gift shops and home stores

TIPS

● Be sure to make a reservation before visiting the area's restaurants; tables fill up fast.
● Dog lovers shouldn't miss the residential blocks' small hidden parks, where canines and their owners congregate nightly.

First occupied by musicians and teachers in the 1850s, the South End had taken a social nose-dive by the end of the 19th century but is now very much back in vogue with young professionals and artists.

Residential It is a lively residential area, whose elegant bow-fronted terraces, many profusely decorated with balustrades and window boxes, line leafy streets and squares. Running through the middle is Tremont Street, where local shops are punctuated by trendy places to eat. There is a broad ethnic mix here and a strong gay community. The South End has a growing number of art galleries, particularly around Harrison and Thayer streets. The neighborhood lies between Huntington Avenue and the Expressway.

The South End's Victorian houses (left and right)

So Wa'? The most rapidly changing area of the South End, however, is the SoWa district (named such because it sits South of Washington Street). Blessed with the hottest new restaurants and cafés—from Union Bar & Grille to Flour Bakery (both ▷ 84)—the area currently has some of the most expensive real estate and most adventurous interior design in the city, but it has still not been entirely gentrified (a fact that locals say lends it an urbane, gritty feel).

By day and by night Walk the neighborhood's parks during the day, admire its rooftops and the tiny gardens in front of its brownstones, visit its trendy art galleries and home goods shops, then stay to enjoy dinner in its stylish restaurants. Spring and summer bring elaborate gardens into bloom and fine alfresco dining.

THE BASICS

www.southend.org
✚ H8
✉ Between the Expressway and Massachusetts Avenue
🕐 Most shops open 10–6. Most restaurants open 5pm–midnight
🍴 Excellent bistros line each side of the street
🚇 Back Bay Station, New England Medical Center
♿ Fair to excellent, depending on the business. Many have elevators

Trinity Church and Copley Square

HIGHLIGHTS

Trinity Church
- Polychrome interior
- John La Farge paintings and lancet windows
- Lantern tower
- Christmas candlelight services

TIP

- Free guided tours are offered most days. Call for the schedule.

H. H. Richardson's prototype French Romanesque church is often described as America's masterpiece of ecclesiastical architecture. It faces Copley Square, bounded by other notable buildings—Boston Public Library and the Fairmont Copley Plaza Hotel.

Trinity Church The Back Bay was a newly developed landfill area when in 1872 Henry Hobson Richardson was commissioned to draw up designs for a new Trinity Church. A massive lantern tower over the transept crossing dominates the church inside and out, requiring more than 2,000 wooden piles massed together to support its granite foundations. Externally, the granite blocks are broken up by bands of pink sandstone. Inside, John La Farge created an intricate

Trinity Church sits alongside its tall neighbor, reflected in the mirrorlike glass (left); detail of the ornate frescos by John La Farge that decorate the walls above the gilded archway in Trinity Church (middle); the contrasting 19th-century and 20th-century architecture (right)

polychrome interior, a tapestry of reds and greens highlighted with gold. The church also contains several important examples of La Farge's ground-breaking stained-glass work. In the baptistery is a bust by Daniel Chester French of the portly rector Phillips Brooks, who composed the carol "O Little Town of Bethlehem."

John Hancock Tower There is something immensely serene about this icy shaft of blue glass. Designed by Henry Cobb, of I. M. Pei & Partners, the building caused a big sensation at first. But it has long since found a place in (most) Bostonians' hearts. After 9/11, the observatory on the 60th floor was closed to the public, for security reasons. But visitors can still admire the tower from the outside, walking around it to see how clearly it reflects the historic buildings nearby.

THE BASICS

Trinity Church
www.trinitychurchboston.org
✚ G6
✉ Copley Square
☎ 617/536-0944
🕐 Daily 8–6
🚇 Copley
♿ Good
✋ Free
❓ Free half-hour organ recitals Fri 12.15. Sun services 7.45, 9, 11.15 (with choir music), 6

John Hancock Tower
✚ H6
✉ Copley Square
🍴 Nearby
🚇 Copley

77

More to See

BACK BAY FENS
Once a saltwater bay, this was the first of Frederick Law Olmsted's string of parks, part of the so-called "Emerald Necklace" of open green spaces. Tall rushes line the banks of the Muddy River behind the Museum of Fine Arts; stroll through the willows or sit in the Rose Garden.

✚ E8 ✉ The Fenway/Park Drive 🚇 Hynes Convention Center, Museum of Fine Arts

CHARLES RIVER ESPLANADE
A favorite for roller blading, jogging, sunbathing, boating and biking. Free summer concerts in Hatch Shell (▷ 83). Also open-air film screenings. Boat tours leave from near the Science Museum.

✚ H5 ✉ Storrow Memorial Drive 🚇 Charles/MGH

FENWAY PARK FOR RED SOX
www.redsox.com

The Boston Red Sox play from April through October. "Friendly Fenway," famous for its Green Monster, the high left-field wall, is the oldest ballpark in the US, although it has been renovated.

✚ E7 ✉ 4 Yawkey Way ☎ Tickets: 877/733-7699. Tours: 617/226-6666 🚇 Kenmore

FIRST CHURCH OF CHRIST, SCIENTIST AND THE MAPPARIUM
www.tfccs.com
www.marybakereddylibrary.org

The scale of this complex is mind-blowing. The world headquarters for the Church of Christ, Scientist, occupies 4 acres (6ha) of prime Back Bay land, with a church seating 3,000. The Mother Church of Christian Science was founded in Boston in 1892 by Mary Baker Eddy. The Mapparium, on the first floor of the Mary Baker Eddy Library, is a brightly colored stained-glass globe, so huge you can walk inside it and stand at the center of the world. It was made in the early 1930s. Try out the echo to get decidedly weird effects.

✚ F7 ✉ 175 Huntington Avenue; Library: 200 Massachusetts Avenue ☎ 617/450-2000 🕐 Church: daily. Library: Tue–Sun 10–4 🚇 Prudential 💷 Library: moderate

A floodlighted Red Sox baseball game at Fenway Park

South End Stroll

You will see Victorian architecture, boutiques, restaurants and parks. Make sure you leave time to stop, browse and snack.

DISTANCE: 1.6 miles (2.5km) **ALLOW:** 3–6 hours

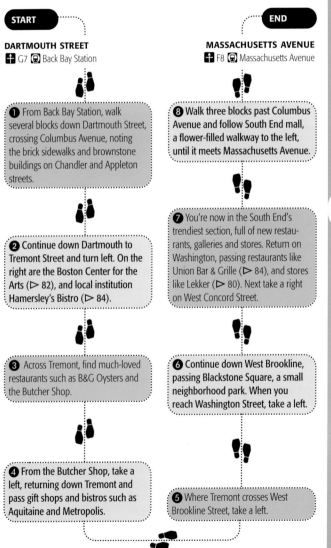

START

DARTMOUTH STREET
🚻 G7 🚇 Back Bay Station

END

MASSACHUSETTS AVENUE
🚻 F8 🚇 Massachusetts Avenue

1 From Back Bay Station, walk several blocks down Dartmouth Street, crossing Columbus Avenue, noting the brick sidewalks and brownstone buildings on Chandler and Appleton streets.

2 Continue down Dartmouth to Tremont Street and turn left. On the right are the Boston Center for the Arts (▷ 82), and local institution Hamersley's Bistro (▷ 84).

3 Across Tremont, find much-loved restaurants such as B&G Oysters and the Butcher Shop.

4 From the Butcher Shop, take a left, returning down Tremont and pass gift shops and bistros such as Aquitaine and Metropolis.

8 Walk three blocks past Columbus Avenue and follow South End mall, a flower-filled walkway to the left, until it meets Massachusetts Avenue.

7 You're now in the South End's trendiest section, full of new restaurants, galleries and stores. Return on Washington, passing restaurants like Union Bar & Grille (▷ 84), and stores like Lekker (▷ 80). Next take a right on West Concord Street.

6 Continue down West Brookline, passing Blackstone Square, a small neighborhood park. When you reach Washington Street, take a left.

5 Where Tremont crosses West Brookline Street, take a left.

Shopping

1154 LILL STUDIO
Handbags are featured here—both ready-to-buy and design-your-own styles are available, with an impressive selection of styles, fabrics and straps. ➕ G6 ✉ 220 Newbury Street ☎ 617/247-1154 🚇 Hynes Convention Center

ALAN BILZERIAN
A fun one for window-shopping (or buying, of course, if you're very rich or very outrageous) for the latest clothes from Rick Owens, Yohji Yamamoto and the like. ➕ H6 ✉ 34 Newbury Street ☎ 617/536-1001 🚇 Arlington

ALLEN EDMONDS
Top-quality shoes in classic styles come in an impressively wide range of sizes. ➕ H6 ✉ 36 Newbury Street ☎ 617/247-3363 🚇 Arlington

AMERICAN APPAREL
Sincere and fashionable, American Apparel is a leader in the anti-sweat-shop movement. Look for all the basics here, with styles that are fun and attractive. Also carries organic clothing. ➕ G6 ✉ 138 Newbury Street ☎ 617/661-2770 🚇 Arlington

ARTFUL HAND
American crafts, including woven silk scarfs, wood-work, ceramics and glass. In Copley Place Mall. ➕ G7 ✉ 36 Copley Place ☎ 617/262-9601 🚇 Copley, Prudential

BARNEYS NEW YORK
A second home to the city's high-spending hip-sters, where you can find of-the-moment labels like 3.1 by Philip Lim and Lanvin. Don't miss the luxurious shoe section anchored by a fireplace. ➕ G7 ✉ 100 Huntington Avenue ☎ 617/385-3300 🚇 Copley

BROOKSTONE
Household, personal and travel equipment here goes well beyond the definition of "gadgets"—useful, high-quality tools for living that you never knew existed. ➕ G7 ✉ 100 Huntington Place ☎ 617/267-4308 🚇 Copley

COPLEY FLAIR
A full stable of stationery and cards, plus novelty pens, gift wrap and

MORE CHOICE
These large outdoor activity stores are all on Commonwealth Avenue.
Eastern Mountain Sports
Hiking, backpacking, camping, mountaineering, cross-country skiing. ✉ 1041 Commonwealth Avenue ☎ 617/254-4250
Ski Market
Skiing, snowboarding, in-line skating, biking. Ski and snowboard rentals. Good children's section. ✉ 860 Commonwealth Avenue ☎ 617/731-6100

assorted other specialty gifts for every holiday. ➕ G6 ✉ 583 Boylston Street ☎ 617/247-1648 🚇 Copley

EMPORIO ARMANI
Slightly less haute couture but more accessible price-wise than Giorgio Armani (No. 22 Newbury Street). The store has a popular café, with outside tables in summer—just the place after some serious shopping. ➕ G6 ✉ 2 Copley Place ☎ 617/262-7300 🚇 Copley

FILENE'S BASEMENT
With little in common (except the crowded racks and narrow aisles) with the beloved old "real" basement at Downtown Crossing, this new incarnation sells off-price high-price without the great values and automatic mark-downs that made the old store fun. ➕ G6 ✉ 497 Boylston Street ☎ 617/424-5520 🚇 Copley

GRETTA LUXE
Find pretty, hard-to-find designs by posh global designers (Barbara Bui and Missoni to Chloe) for women, *plus chic* (and *très chère*) hand-bags and shoes. ➕ G7 ✉ 10 Huntington Avenue ☎ 617/536-1959 🚇 Copley

LEKKER
"Lekker" is a Dutch word meaning alluring and attractive. This South End

store sells unique European home accessories and furniture.
✚ G9 ✉ 1317 Washington Street ☎ 617/542-6464 Ⓠ Union Park Street

LUSH

This shop bursts with fragrance and friendliness, as well as with vibrant color. Handmade soaps and other earth-kind cosmetics are bright, unusual, nicely packaged and reasonably priced. These make good easy-to-pack gifts.
✚ G6 ✉ 166 Newbury Street ☎ 617/375-5874 Ⓠ Copley

MARC JACOBS

The celebrated American designer showcases both his more expensive and casual lines at this funky but posh boutique. Duck in to find women's coats, dresses, pants (trousers) and skirts, plus accessories and home decor.
✚ G6 ✉ 81 Newbury Street ☎ 617/425-0707 Ⓠ Copley

MATSU

Chic gifts and (a few) clothes, many Asian.
✚ G6 ✉ 259 Newbury Street ☎ 617/266-9707 Ⓠ Copley, Hynes Convention Center

NEWBURY COMICS

The hippest record shop in town. CDs, T-shirts, posters and comics.
✚ G6 ✉ 332 Newbury Street ☎ 617/236-4930 Ⓠ Hynes Convention Center

NIKETOWN

Large, state-of-the-art store, arranged by pavilion: men's and women's shoes for training and running, golf, basketball, soccer, tennis and more.
✚ G6 ✉ 200 Newbury Street ☎ 617/267-3400 Ⓠ Copley

PIERRE DEUX

French fabrics, wallpapers, table linens and lampshades.
✚ G6 ✉ 111 Newbury Street ☎ 617/536-6364 Ⓠ Arlington

POTTERY BARN

Stylish accessories and furniture.
✚ G6 ✉ 122 Newbury Street ☎ 617/266-6553 Ⓠ Arlington

PRUDENTIAL CENTER

A dozen clothes stores (including Chico's, Ann Taylor, J. Jill and Olympia Sports), some shoe and accessories shops, gift and specialty (such as Crane's stationery) stores and a hardware store. Also home to department stores Saks Fifth Avenue and Lord & Taylor, a post office, ATMs, a superb food court and Legal Sea Foods.
✚ G7 ✉ Between Boylston Street and Huntington Avenue 🕐 Mon–Sat 10–9, Sun 11–6 Ⓠ Prudential

SECOND TIME AROUND

Not your usual thrift shop, this resale shop specializes in better brands and higher quality. But it's more accessible than the traditional Junior League designer resale shops. You never know what you'll find here.
✚ G6 ✉ 176 Newbury Street ☎ 617/247-3504 Ⓠ Copley

SIMON PEARCE

Exquisite handmade art glass and utilitarian glassware beautiful enough to be decorator pieces. Simon Pearce is a well-known New England artist.
✚ G6 ✉ 115 Newbury Street ☎ 617/450-8388 Ⓠ Arlington

WILLIAMS-SONOMA

For the cook who has everything—or so you thought until you came in here: from Dualit toasters and heart-shaped muffin baking trays to French table linens.
✚ G7 ✉ Copley Place ☎ 617/262-5892 Ⓠ Copley

BACK BAY AND THE SOUTH END

🎁 **SHOPPING**

Entertainment and Nightlife

28 DEGREES
www.28degrees-boston.com
The chic South End lounge, known for its martinis, is next to the long-time favorite restaurant, Icarus. The varied menu features small plates, platters, brick-oven pizzas and raw shellfish. Great vibe.
H7 ⊠ 1 Appleton Street
☎ 617/728-0728 Ⓜ Back Bay Station

BERKLEE PERFORMANCE CENTER
www.berkleebpc.com
This Back Bay venue seats 1,220 and hosts jazz, pop, folk and world music concerts by international performers and by the students and staff of the Berklee College of Music.
F7 ⊠ 136 Massachusetts Avenue ☎ 617/747–2261
Ⓜ Hynes Convention Center

BLEACHER BAR
www.bleacherbarboston.com
The ultimate sports bar inside Fenway Park's Green Monster. Small and crowded at game time, the field level view looks across center field to home plate. Basic beer and pub food, but the view is the real star here.
E7 ⊠ 82 Lansdowne Street ☎ 617/262-2424
Ⓜ Kenmore

BOSTON BEER WORKS
www.beerworks.net
Sports bar and microbrewery with hand-crafted ales, lagers, stouts and pilsners on tap. Upscale bar food like pan-roasted salmon, stir-fries and burgers. Located near Fenway Park, so expect crowds when the Red Sox are playing.
E7 ⊠ 61 Brookline Avenue ☎ 617/536-2337
Ⓜ Kenmore

BOSTON CENTER FOR THE ARTS
www.bcaonline.org
Three stages at this South End performance space house several contemporary theater companies, including the provocative Company One and the cutting-edge SpeakEasy Stage Company.
H7 ⊠ 539 Tremont Street ☎ 617/426-5000 Ⓜ Back Bay Station

BOSTON PUBLIC LIBRARY
www.bpl.org
The occasional film series usually features

> ### BLUE LAWS
> The legacy of the Puritans continues in strict state laws to curtail imbibing. Most bars in Boston and Cambridge close at 1am during the week, and 2am on the weekends—though you may find restaurants in Chinatown that still serve later. Happy-hour specials, such as 2-for-1 drinks, are also prohibited, though some bars serve free appetizers after work.

lesser-known old films.
G7 ⊠ Copley Square
☎ 617/536-5400
Ⓜ Copley

BUKOWSKI TAVERN
More than 100 varieties of suds are on offer at this friendly and unpretentious spot. The beer drinker in your group will be in heaven.
F7 ⊠ 50 Dalton Street
☎ 617/437-9999 Ⓜ Hynes Convention Center

CASK 'N FLAGON
www.casknflagon.com
The perfect pit-stop before, during and after a Red Sox game, this rowdy sports bar has enough big-screen TVs to please the biggest fan.
D7 ⊠ 62 Brookline Avenue ☎ 617/536-4840
Ⓜ Kenmore

CITY-BAR
www.citybarboston.com
Ultradim lighting and a stellar martini list makes this cool little hideaway inside the Lenox Hotel perfect for a mysterious rendezvous.
G6 ⊠ 61 Exeter Street
☎ 617/933-4800 Ⓜ Copley, Back Bay Station

CLUB CAFÉ
www.clubcafe.com
A nightly playground for the gay and lesbian crowd, this upscale lounge, restaurant and "video bar" literally has something—and somebody—for everyone.
H7 ⊠ 209 Columbus

Avenue ☎ 617/536-0966
🚇 Back Bay Station

DELUX CAFE
Christmas lights, Elvis
statues and Dr. Seuss
wallpaper in the bath-
rooms. The interior here
is as eclectic as its
clientele. Try the tasty
bar menu.
➕ H7 ✉ 100 Chandler Street
☎ 617/338-5258 🚇 Back Bay
Station

HATCH SHELL
www.state.ma.us/mdc
The Boston Pops
Orchestra gives free
concerts here in early
July. The highlight is the
concert with fireworks
on July 4. Other musical
groups perform through-
out the summer.
➕ H5 ✉ Esplanade,
Embankment Road
☎ 617/626-4970
🚇 Charles/MGH, Arlington

HOUSE OF BLUES
BOSTON
www.houseofblues.com
Live blues, rhythm and
blues, jazz, rock and
gospel. Also a theater,
private lounge and restaurant. Gospel brunch buf-
fet on Sunday is popular.
➕ E7 ✉ 15 Lansdowne
Street ☎ 888/693-2583
🚇 Kenmore

HUNTINGTON
THEATER COMPANY
www.bu.edu/huntington
Performances from
Boston University's resi-
dent professional troupe
include European and

American, classical and
modern, comedies and
musicals.
➕ F7 ✉ 264 Huntington
Avenue ☎ 617/266-0800
🚇 Symphony

JILLIAN'S
www.jilliansboston.com
Virtual sports, 200 high-
tech games, 50 pool
tables, plus five bars and
bistro-style food.
➕ E7 ✉ 145 Ipswich Street
☎ 617/437-0300 🕐 Daily
11am–2am 🚇 Kenmore

JORDAN HALL
www.necmusic.edu
This glittering and acousti-
cally perfect venue, in the
prestigious New England
Conservatory, showcases
the resident Boston
Philharmonic, Boston
Baroque and Cantata
Singers. Conservatory
students perform free

concerts year-round.
➕ E8 ✉ 30 Gainsborough
Street, one block west of
Symphony Hall ☎ 617/585-
1260 🚇 Symphony

KINGS
www.kingsbackbay.com
This subterranean spot
has the latest electronic
scoring equipment. Relax
in the hipster lounge after
you tire of rolling strikes
or gutter-balls.
➕ F7 ✉ 50 Dalton Street
☎ 617/266-2695 🚇 Hynes
Convention Center

MUSEUM OF FINE
ARTS
www.mfa.org/film/
International, early and
offbeat films.
➕ E8 ✉ 465 Huntington
Avenue ☎ 617/267-9300
🚇 Museum of Fine Arts

SYMPHONY HALL
www.bso.org
"Symphony" is home to
the renowned Boston
Symphony Orchestra
from September through
May. The orchestra often
performs on Friday after-
noon, Saturday, Tuesday
and Thursday evenings.
Call for current schedule,
as performance days vary
month-to-month. The
Boston Pops Orchestra
concerts are held here in
December, May and June
before moving to the
Hatch Shell (▷ left) in
July.
➕ F7 ✉ 301 Massachusetts
Avenue ☎ Box office 617/266-
1200; general information
617/266-1492 🚇 Symphony

Restaurants

BRASSERIE JO ($$–$$$)

www.brasseriejo.com
Opposite the Prudential Center, this traditional French brasserie specializes in Alsatian dishes, but serves all the French faves, from onion tart to coq au vin. Desserts are knockouts.

✚ G7 ✉ 120 Huntington Avenue ☎ 617/425-3240 🕒 Breakfast, lunch, dinner daily 🚇 Prudential

CASA ROMERO ($$)

Authentic, upscale Mexican dining. Generous portions of dishes including the signature tenderloin of pork marinated in oranges and smoked chipotle peppers.

✚ F6 ✉ 30 Gloucester Street ☎ 617/536-4341 🕒 Dinner daily 🚇 Hynes Convention Center

CLIO ($$$)

www.eliothotel.com
Excellent fare that's creative without being weird. Good seafood preparations include chilled lobster and scallops with hot-and-sour bell-pepper broth. The sashimi bar is excellent.

✚ F6 ✉ Eliot Hotel, 370a Commonwealth Avenue, Back Bay ☎ 617/536-7200 🕒 Breakfast daily, dinner Tue–Sun 🚇 Hynes Convention Center

L'ESPALIER ($$$)

www.lespalier.com
Superb contemporary fare in the formal setting of a 19th-century Back Bay house. Prix fixe.

✚ F6 ✉ 774 Boylston Street, Back Bay ☎ 617/262-3023 🕒 Lunch, dinner daily 🚇 Hynes Convention Center

HAMERSLEY'S BISTRO ($$$)

www.hamersleybistro.com
Excellent American-French dishes; try roast chicken with garlic and lemon.

✚ H7 ✉ 553 Tremont Street (at Clarendon), South End ☎ 617/423-2700 🕒 Dinner daily 🚇 Back Bay Station

HARU ($$$)

www.harusushi.com
This smartly styled restaurant offers not just exemplary sushi, but tempura that melts in the mouth and a sophisticated menu of favorites along with

inspired new creations.

✚ G7 ✉ 55 Huntington Avenue ☎ 617/536-0770 🕒 Lunch, dinner daily 🚇 Prudential

ICARUS ($$$)

www.icarusrestaurant.com
Seasonal ingredients make up a sophisticated menu that might include chestnut-stuffed pork or ribeye in sour-cherry port sauce. Three-course chef's tasting menus are good value.

✚ H7 ✉ 3 Appleton Street, South End ☎ 617/426-1790 🕒 Dinner daily 🚇 Back Bay Station

PETIT ROBERT BISTRO ($$)

www.petitrobertbistro.com
A bistro in the truest Parisian sense, serving serious foods at sensible prices. Look for unusual ingredients and perfectly seared foie gras. Sit at the downstairs dessert bar to watch the pastry chef create your dessert.

✚ E6 ✉ 468 Commonwealth Avenue ☎ 617/375-0699 🕒 Lunch, dinner daily 🚇 Kenmore

UNION BAR & GRILLE ($$)

www.unionrestaurant.com
Stylish and often packed bar/restaurant, serving big plates of burgers and house-cured duck confit.

✚ Off map at G9 ✉ 1357 Washington Street ☎ 617/423-0555 🕒 Dinner daily, brunch Sat–Sun 🚇 Back Bay Station

This historic and multicultural city across the river from Boston is one of America's greatest academic centers, thanks to universities such as Harvard and the Massachusetts Institute of Technology.

Sights	88–92	Top 25	**TOP 25**
Walk	93	Harvard Square and Harvard University ▷ 88	
Shopping	94–95	Harvard University Museums ▷ 90	
Entertainment and Nightlife	96–97		
Restaurants	97–98		

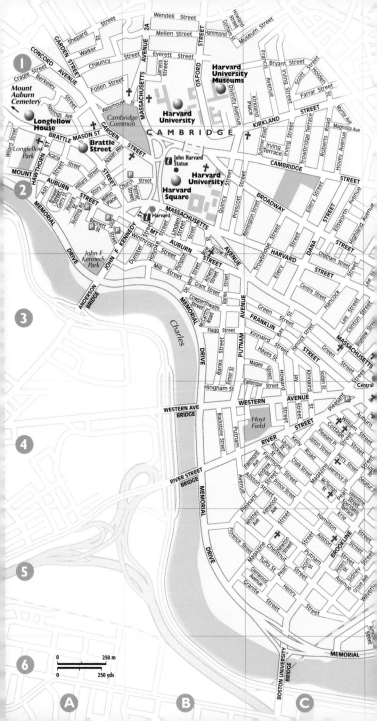

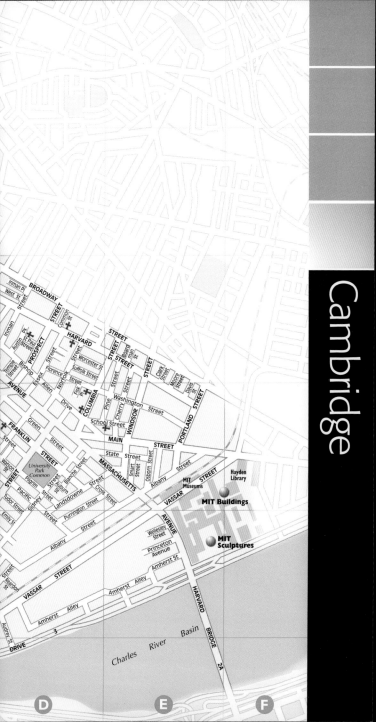

Cambridge

INMAN Pl
West Street
Inman
BROADWAY
Temple
Bishop Allen Drive
AUSTIN Street
PROSPECT St Paul Street
Common St
STREET
HARVARD
STREET
Worcester St
Essex Street
Florence Street
Suffolk Street
Norfolk Street
Allen
COLUMBIA
Fisk Pl
Pine Street
Cherry Street
Washington
Board man St
Clark Street
Moore Street
Davis Street
PORTLAND STREET
School Street
WINDSOR
Street
AVENUE
FRANKLIN
Green Street
STREET
State Street
MAIN
STREET
Auburn
Blanche Street
Smart Street
Osborn Street
Albany Street
VASSAR STREET
MASSACHUSETTS
MIT Museums
Hayden Library
University Park Common
STREET
Pacific Street
Sidney Street
Landsdowne Street
Cross Street
Street
MIT Buildings
Pilgrim Street
Waverly Street
Tudor Street
Emily St
Purrington Street
Wellesley Street
AVENUE
Princeton Avenue
MIT Sculptures
Albany
Amherst St
Street
Pearson St
VASSAR STREET
Amherst Alley
Amherst Alley
HARVARD
Audrey St
DRIVE
Charles River Basin
BRIDGE
2A

D   E   F

Harvard Square and Harvard University

HIGHLIGHTS

- Harvard Yard
- Radcliffe Yard
- Browsing in a bookshop all evening

TIPS

- Harvard is one place where a guided tour is essential. Stop in the Holyoke Arcade at 1350 Massachusetts Avenue to sign up for a free one.
- Stroll down to the river to watch the crew teams practice.

One of the most significant strands in the fabric of Bostonian life is the academic scene. In Cambridge you can walk through hallowed Harvard Yard in the footsteps of the great, then enjoy the funky scene in Harvard Square.

Harvard University Among the first things the Massachusetts Bay colonists did was to provide for the training of ministers, and thus was founded, in 1636, what became one of the world's most respected seats of learning. Most of its historic buildings are in Harvard Yard, entered across the street from the First Parish Church. Ahead, in front of Bulfinch's granite University Hall, is a statue by Daniel Chester French of benefactor John Harvard.

The elegant 18th-century redbrick halls grouped around this, the Old Yard, are dormitories. Behind

Clockwise from left: A café in Harvard Square; students gather around the ornate gateway into a Harvard college; students on lawns outside Widener Memorial Library; a street-musician entertains in Harvard Square; New Yard in the fall; pedestrians and students mingle in Harvard Square

University Hall is New Yard, with Memorial Church on the left facing the pillared facade of Widener Library. Pass beside H. H. Richardson's Sever Hall to emerge in Quincy Street opposite the Carpenter Center for the Visual Arts, the only Le Corbusier building in North America. The Fogg Art Museum (▷ 91) is next door. Radcliffe Institute is alongside Cambridge Common, around the lovely Radcliffe Yard.

Harvard Square The newsstand by the T is a famous landmark in this "square," which is actually more of a district than a square. Here you can watch chess, listen to street musicians, sit in an outdoor café, eat dessert at any time of day in Finale (30 Dunster Street), shop for trendy clothes, browse in bookshops or go to a club for jazz or reggae.

THE BASICS

www.harvard.edu
➕ B1/B2
✉ Harvard University: Harvard Yard, Peabody Street
☎ City of Cambridge Visitor Information Booth: 617/497-1630; University: 617/495-1573
🕑 Daily
🍴 Plenty
Ⓗ Harvard
♿ Free
❓ Campus tours Mon–Fri 10, 2, Sat 2

UNIVERSITY MUSEUM

Harvard University Museums

The facade of the Museum of Natural History (left); displays (below and right)

Few universities have such an enviable collection. The pieces in Harvard's three art museums, each of which has its own character, are of world-class quality.

Fogg Art Museum Concentration is on Italian early-Renaissance art, with artists such as Simone Martini, Bernardo Daddi and Filippo Lippi.

Busch-Reisinger Museum Expressionist art of Central and Northern Europe features, with Bauhaus objects and work by Kandinsky and Klee.

Arthur M. Sackler Museum One of the world's best Chinese jade collections where Chinese bronzes, Japanese prints and Greco-Roman antiquities are the highlights.

Renovations During reconstruction of the Fogg, due for completion in 2013, full collections will not be shown. Selections from it and the Busch-Reisinger will be shown temporarily at the Sackler.

Harvard Museum of Natural History (HMNH) More than 3,000 models of 830 plant species are all so realistic you cannot believe they are made of glass. Elsewhere are wild animals and birds, plus rocks and minerals, including precious gems.

Peabody Museum One of the world's finest collections recording human culture, especially strong in Native American peoples, is interpreted to provide historical and cultural backgrounds. The museum shop is a treasure trove.

THE BASICS

www.harvard.edu/museums

➕ B1

✉ Fogg & Busch-Reisinger: 32 Quincy Street. Sackler: 485 Broadway. HMNH: 26 Oxford Street. Peabody: 11 Divinity Avenue

☎ Art museums: 617/495-9400. HMNH: 617/495-3045. Peabody: 617/496-1027

🕐 Art museums: Mon–Sat 10–5, Sun 1–5. HMNH and Peabody: daily 9–5

♿ Very good

💲 Moderate. Art museums free Sat am. HMNH and Peabody free to Massachusetts residents Sep–May Wed pm, all year Sun am. CityPass applies

HIGHLIGHTS

- Impressionists (Fogg)
- Jade (Sackler)
- Glass flowers (HMNH)
- Native American exhibits (Peabody)

More to See

LONGFELLOW HOUSE AND BRATTLE STREET
In the pre-Revolutionary 1770s the land on either side of Brattle Street was owned by loyalist families, forced to quit when the Patriots took over the area in 1774. Henry Wadsworth Longfellow came to No. 105 Longfellow Street as a lodger in 1837 and wrote many of his poems here. Take the tour through the house, including, of course, Longfellow's study.
✚ A1/A2 ✉ 105 Brattle Street ☎ 617/876-4492 ◷ Mid-Jun to mid-Oct Wed–Sun 10–4.30 🚇 Harvard, then pleasant walk (0.5 miles/0.8km) 💷 Inexpensive

MIT BUILDINGS
http://web.mit.edu
MIT has some impressive modern architecture. You are free to wander around the campus. Seek out Eero Saarinen's serene round chapel (1955). Don't miss Frank Gehry's latest whimsical Ray and Maria Stata Center for Computer, Information and Intelligence Sciences (2004), on Vassar Street. On and near Ames Street the low Wiesner and the tall Green buildings are the work of I. M. Pei (1964, 1985).
✚ E4 ✉ Massachusetts Avenue, Vassar Street, Ames Street 🚇 Kendall 💷 Free

MIT SCULPTURES
On the campus are two Henry Moore reclining figure pieces (1963, 1976), Alexander Calder's black steel *The Big Sail* (1965) and Michael Heizer's pink granite *Guennette* (1977).
✚ E5 ✉ Memorial Drive ◷ Daily 🚇 Kendall 💷 Free

MOUNT AUBURN CEMETERY
A little out of the way, but a beautiful place. It was built in 1831 as the country's first rural garden cemetery and is still very popular with bird and plant lovers. If it's a nice day you could walk from Longfellow House. Longfellow now rests here, as does the artist Winslow Homer.
✚ Off map at A1 ✉ 580 Mount Auburn Street ☎ 617/547-7105 ◷ Daily 🚇 Harvard, then walk or Watertown bus

Mount Auburn Cemetery

Portrait of Henry Wadsworth Longfellow

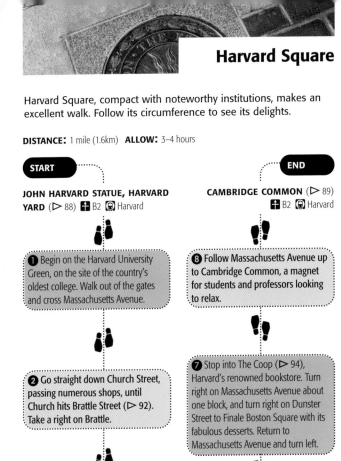

Harvard Square

Harvard Square, compact with noteworthy institutions, makes an excellent walk. Follow its circumference to see its delights.

DISTANCE: 1 mile (1.6km) **ALLOW:** 3–4 hours

START

JOHN HARVARD STATUE, HARVARD YARD (▷ 88) ✚ B2 Ⓜ Harvard

END

CAMBRIDGE COMMON (▷ 89) ✚ B2 Ⓜ Harvard

❶ Begin on the Harvard University Green, on the site of the country's oldest college. Walk out of the gates and cross Massachusetts Avenue.

❷ Go straight down Church Street, passing numerous shops, until Church hits Brattle Street (▷ 92). Take a right on Brattle.

❸ Continue down Brattle Street, passing stately mansions, on the way to the Longfellow House (▷ 92), where Henry Wadsworth Longfellow once lived.

❹ Turn around on Brattle and head back toward Harvard Square, passing the American Repertory Theatre (▷ 96) on the way.

❽ Follow Massachusetts Avenue up to Cambridge Common, a magnet for students and professors looking to relax.

❼ Stop into The Coop (▷ 94), Harvard's renowned bookstore. Turn right on Massachusetts Avenue about one block, and turn right on Dunster Street to Finale Boston Square with its fabulous desserts. Return to Massachusetts Avenue and turn left.

❻ Farther up, pass the Brattle Theatre (▷ 96), an independent cinema and one of the Square's most revered cultural stops. Follow Brattle to the left, where it meets up with Massachusetts Avenue.

❺ In the last blocks of Brattle, duck into the row's unique stores and gift shops.

CAMBRIDGE

WALK

93

Shopping

ABODEON
A stockpile of modern and retro housewares. The vintage furniture is particularly impressive, though you may also want to pick up a few pieces of tableware (from local and global makers) while you're at it.
➕ Off map at B1 ✉ 1731 Massachusetts Avenue ☎ 617/497-0137 🚇 Harvard

BEADWORKS
A well-organized little one-room shop filled with small bins of everything you need to make your own jewelry—semi-precious stones, ceramic beads, clasps, wire and more.
➕ B2 ✉ 23 Church Street ☎ 617/868-9777 🚇 Harvard

CAMBRIDGE ANTIQUE MARKET
Another large Cambridge cooperative. Dealers sell china, glass, quilts, clothes, silver, jewelry and collectibles.
➕ Off map at G3 ✉ 201 Monsignor O'Brien Highway, diagonally opposite the Lechmere T ☎ 617/868-9655 🕐 Closed Mon 🚇 Lechmere

CAMBRIDGE ARTISTS' COOPERATIVE
Quilts, weaving, jewelry, scarves—all made locally.
➕ B2 ✉ 59a Church Street ☎ 617/868-4434 🚇 Harvard

CARDULLO'S
www.cardullos.com
Crammed with international specialty foods, first-rate baked goods and the fixings for gift baskets, this family-run fixture is the place to pick up all your favorite foods and ingredients.
➕ A2 ✉ 6 Brattle Street ☎ 617/491-8888 🚇 Harvard

CURIOUS GEORGE GOES TO WORDSWORTH
WordsWorth's children's bookshop, full of delights.
➕ B2 ✉ 1 JFK Street ☎ 617/498-0062 🚇 Harvard

GLOBE CORNER BOOKSTORE
One of the largest selections of books and maps for travelers. Browse for guidebooks, recreation guides, travel literature and books on photography, cooking and language. An exceptional variety of atlases, globes, destination maps and historical maps.
➕ B2 ✉ 90 Mount Auburn Street ☎ 617/497-6277 🚇 Harvard

BOOKSTORES
Cambridge, and Harvard Square in particular, has an amazing concentration of independent bookshops; just a handful are mentioned here. Pick up a complete guide from the information kiosk by Harvard Square T. Chainstores such as Borders and Barnes & Noble are to be found throughout Boston and Cambridge.

GROLIER POETRY BOOKSHOP
The US's only shop devoted entirely to poetry.
➕ B2 ✉ 6 Plympton Street ☎ 617/547-4648 🚇 Harvard

HARVARD BOOKSTORE
Known for academic titles and other nonfiction. New and used books.
➕ B2 ✉ 1256 Massachusetts Avenue ☎ 617/661-1515 🚇 Harvard

HARVARD COOP
A peaceful oasis of children's books in the store's basement. A calm, quiet place to browse.
➕ B2 ✉ 1400 Massachusetts Avenue ☎ 617/499-2000 🚇 Harvard

HARVARD SQUARE
Cambridge's Harvard Square is a maze of streets with dozens of bookshops (many stay open all evening), music shops and clothes stores, (new and secondhand) much of it geared for students. It's an entertaining place, too, with a wide variety of restaurants and cafés. Check out Brattle Street, Church Street, Eliot Street (with the Charles Square complex just off), JFK Street and Dunster Street. As some of the chains have moved into the area, so some of the smaller local shops have moved, or opened up, just north of Harvard and there's now a clutch of funky clothes and gift

shops on Massachusetts Avenue heading toward Porter Square.

HIDDEN SWEETS
There's a lot more than candy inside, although you'll find the traditional "Boston Baked Beans" and maple sweets. Look here for lower prices on Harvard and Red Sox insignia items, and for smart-alec pins, bumper stickers and notepapers that proclaim your progressive politics.
🚹 B2 ✉ 25 Brattle Street ☎ 617/497-2600 🚇 Harvard

LEAVITT & PIERCE INC.
A 120-year-old tobacco shop peddling bins of tobacco, pipes, men's shaving supplies and vintage chess sets.
🚹 B2 ✉ 1316 Massachusetts Avenue ☎ 617/547-0576 🚇 Harvard

MDF
Modern Designer Furnishings: finely crafted picture frames, vases, serving pieces, lamps and small tables.
🚹 A2 ✉ 19 Brattle Street ☎ 617/491-2789 🚇 Harvard

MINT JULEP
Attractive, stylish, but accessible and timeless clothing in luscious fabrics and colors are the style here. Accessories are equally well chosen, and the staff is helpful.
🚹 B2 ✉ 6 Church Street ☎ 617/576-6468 🚇 Harvard

NEWBURY COMICS
Music, especially rock & roll, sold as CDs, DVDs, LPs and singles. Look for pop culture merchandise, including comics, posters, T-shirts and much more.
🚹 B2 ✉ 36 JFK Street ☎ 617/491-0337 🚇 Harvard

NOMAD
Baskets handmade in Mexico, Asian masks, carved wooden switch-plates from Brazil and jewelry and clothing from Europe—the global market makes its way to the colorful shelves of Nomad.
🚹 Off map at B1 ✉ 1741 Massachusetts Avenue ☎ 617/497-6677 🚇 Porter

SCHOENHOF'S FOREIGN BOOKS
For more than 150 years Schoenhof's has offered foreign-language books. There are thousands of books, including classics in original Greek or Latin, contemporary literature, poetry, philosophy, children's books and language materials.

French, German, Italian and Spanish titles are featured, with hundreds of other languages represented as well.
🚹 B2 ✉ 76A Mount Auburn Street ☎ 617/547-8855 🚇 Harvard

STELLABELLA TOYS
This shop repeatedly wins awards for its selection of first-class, imaginative playthings.
🚹 C2 ✉ 1360 Cambridge Street ☎ 617/491-6290 🚇 Central

TESS & CARLOS
Stylish, classic clothes, shoes and accessories for men and women. The cashmere sweater collection and racks of apparel by Italian designers are particularly impressive.
🚹 A2 ✉ 20 Brattle Street ☎ 617/846-8377 🚇 Harvard

URBAN OUTFITTERS
Where the young come to get that rugged look. Funky household goods.
🚹 B2 ✉ 11 JFK Street ☎ 617/864-0070 🚇 Harvard

VIA VAI
Fine women's clothing, from international as well as local designers. Also a small but tasteful selection of accessories.
🚹 B2 ✉ 63 JFK Street ☎ 617/497-9959 🚇 Harvard

CAMBRIDGE

SHOPPING

Entertainment and Nightlife

AMERICAN REPERTORY THEATRE
www.amrep.org
A highly regarded professional repertory company based in Harvard Square, staging classical and original drama.
🚼 A2 ✉ Loeb Drama Center, 64 Brattle Street
☎ 617/547-8300 🚇 Harvard

BRATTLE THEATRE
www.brattlefilm.org
Vintage films and film festivals attract connoisseurs to this small, one-screen theater.
🚼 A2 ✉ 40 Brattle Street
☎ 617/876-6837 🚇 Harvard

CANTAB LOUNGE
www.cantab-lounge.com
Neighborhood gathering spot, bar and grill, Cantab offers two venues with nightly performances of an eclectic variety of music and spoken word events. Monday night is Open Mike night in the upstairs lounge.
🚼 C3 ✉ 738 Massachusetts Avenue ☎ 617/354-2685
🚇 Central

CLUB PASSIM
www.clubpassim.com
The Cambridge area's premier folk music venue attracts both up-and-coming and established performers.
🚼 B2 ✉ 47 Palmer Street
☎ 617/492-7679 🚇 Harvard

GREEN STREET
www.greenstreetgrill.com
Varied menu featuring seasonal entrées in a comfortable atmosphere. The cocktail menu is extensive, with fine wines and craft beers that make this neighborhood fixture a popular place to imbibe.
🚼 D4 ✉ 280 Green Street ☎ 617/876-1655
🕐 Dinner daily from 5.30pm
🚇 Central, then short walk

HARPER'S FERRY
www.harpersferryboston.com
Local, regional and national blues and roots rock performers continue to keep this casual place hopping.
🚼 B2 ✉ 156 Brighton Avenue ☎ 617/254-9743
🚇 Harvard

HARVARD FILM ARCHIVE
http://hcl.harvard.edu/hfa
Daily showings of cult and independent films at Harvard's Carpenter Center for the Visual Arts.
🚼 B2 ✉ 24 Quincy Street
☎ 617/495-4700 🚇 Harvard

HASTY PUDDING THEATER
www.hastypudding.org
Home to the touring Hasty Pudding Theatricals company and to the American Repertory Theatre's annual "New Stages" series of contemporary plays.
🚼 B2 ✉ 12 Holyoke Street
☎ 617/495-5205 🚇 Harvard

JOSÉ MATEO'S BALLET THEATRE
Directed by José Mateo, this notable professional company performs a community-friendly mix of classical and contemporary ballet.
🚼 B2 ✉ 400 Harvard Street
☎ 617/354-7467 🚇 Harvard

THE MIDDLE EAST
www.mideastclub.com
The premier venue for alternative rock for not only Cambridge, but also Boston. The Middle Eastern restaurant has three rooms for performers—upstairs, downstairs and in the restaurant.
🚼 C3 ✉ 472/480 Massachusetts Avenue
☎ 617/864-3278 🚇 Central

NOIR BAR
Sophisticated and sultry, this hip nook in the Charles Hotel provides comfortable wrap-around couches for a late-night (2am) martini or

---

ALTERNATIVE DANCE
Contemporary and ethnic dance troupes perform at venues all over the city and beyond. In Boston, these include the **Boston Dance Alliance** (✉ 19 Clarendon Street ☎ 617/456-6295; www.bostondancealliance.org). In Cambridge, look for the **Multicultural Arts Center** (✉ 41 2nd Street ☎ 617/577-1400; www.cmacusa.org) and the **Dance Complex** (✉ 536 Massachusetts Avenue ☎ 617/547-9363; www.dancecomplex.org).

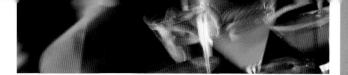

seasonal cocktail seven days a week.

⊞ B2 ✉ 1 Bennett Street ☎ 617/661-8010 🚇 Harvard

REGATTABAR

www.regattabarjazz.com
First-class jazz acts come to Harvard Square at this classy bar in The Charles Hotel (▷ 112).

⊞ A2 ✉ 1 Bennett Street ☎ 617/864-1200 or 617/876-7777 🕐 Closed Mon 🚇 Harvard

RYLES

www.rylesjazz.com
Another Cambridge hot spot, in Inman Square,

with food downstairs. Emphasis is on Latin jazz. Weekly learn-to-salsa Latin dance night.

A BIT OF VARIETY

Fans of old-time vaudeville might like to take a trip out of Boston to Beverly, where Le Grand David and His Own Spectacular Magic Company offer good old-fashioned entertainment at:

Cabot Street Cinema Theater

✉ 286 Cabot Street ☎ 978/927-3677 🕐 Most Sundays

⊞ E3 ✉ 212 Hampshire Street ☎ 617/876-9330 🕐 Music: Tue–Sun from 8.30pm, Sun jazz brunch: 10–3 🚇 Central then long walk or bus 83; Harvard then bus 69 along Cambridge Street

SANDERS THEATRE

www.fas.harvard.edu
A 1,200-seat neo-Gothic theater at Harvard, with classical and world music. Despite its size the 180-degree stage design allows an imtimate feel.

⊞ B2 ✉ Quincy Street at Cambridge Street ☎ 617/496-2222 🚇 Harvard

Restaurants

PRICES

Prices are approximate, based on a 3-course meal for one person.

$$$ over $40
$$ $20–$40
$ under $20

THE BLUE ROOM ($$$)

www.theblueroom.net
This off-the-beaten-track restaurant is one of the best in Boston. The menu changes frequently, offers a creative wine list and features eclectic entrées such as tuna with star anise and ginger, skirt steak, pizza and a nightly

vegetarian option.

⊞ F3 ✉ 1 Kendall Square ☎ 617/494-9034 🕐 Dinner daily, brunch Sun 🚇 Kendall

BORDER CAFÉ ($)

Fun, friendly and crowded, this popular restaurant serves large portions of tasty Cajun and Tex-Mex favorites, including fajitas, tacos, jambalaya and margaritas.

⊞ B2 ✉ 32 Church Street ☎ 617/864-6100 🕐 Lunch, dinner daily (till late) 🚇 Harvard

CASABLANCA ($$)

This restaurant is a popular hangout for Harvard folk and young

professionals, and serves good appetizers and Mediterranean fare.

⊞ A2 ✉ 40 Brattle Street ☎ 617/876-0999 🕐 Lunch, dinner daily 🚇 Harvard

CHEZ HENRI ($–$$)

www.chezhenri.com
Cuban flavors meet classic French dishes in Cambridge's funky, chic bistro. The dining room serves a full menu of sophisticated dishes on one side, while the bar offers excellent Cuban sandwiches and cocktails on the other.

⊞ A1 ✉ 1 Shephard Street ☎ 617/354-8980 🕐 Dinner daily 🚇 Harvard

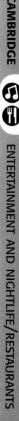

CHRISTINA'S ($)

Christina's homemade ice cream and sorbet draw crowds. An ever-changing menu of flavors ranging from ordinary to unusual, such as burnt sugar, avocado, cardamom and bergamot.

D2 ⊠ 1255 Cambridge Street ☎ 617/492-7021 ⏰ Daily ⓠ Harvard

CRAIGIE ON MAIN ($$$)

www.craigieonmain.com
The menu is so interesting and tempting that regulars opt for the "Chef's Whim" four- or six-course tasting menus offered Wednesday and Sunday after 9pm. Dishes at this exceptionally good bistro have only the freshest local ingredients.

D4 ⊠ 853 Main Street ☎ 617/497-5511 ⏰ Dinner daily, brunch Sun ⓠ Central

HI-RISE ($)

Alfresco coffee and good pastries in Harvard Square's Blacksmith House. Built 1811, this was inspiration for Henry Wadsworth Longfellow's poem "Village Blacksmith."

A2 ⊠ 56 Brattle Street ☎ 617/492-3003 ⏰ Breakfast, lunch daily ⓠ Harvard

L. A. BURDICK CHOCOLATE ($)

www.burdickchocolate.com
If heaven were a chocolate shop it might look something like this café.

A2 ⊠ 52 Brattle Street
☎ 617/491-4340 ⏰ Daily ⓠ Harvard

LEGAL SEA FOODS ($$)

www.legalseafoods.com
Popular seafood chain serving good fish.

F4 ⊠ 5 Cambridge Center, Kendall Square ☎ 617/864-3400 ⏰ Lunch, dinner daily ⓠ Kendall

MR. BARTLEY'S BURGER COTTAGE ($)

Choose from more than two dozen burgers with sweet potato fries, plus salads, sandwiches and desserts.

B2 ⊠ 1246 Massachusetts Avenue ☎ 617/354-6559 ⏰ Lunch, dinner Mon–Sat. Closed Sun ⓠ Harvard

OM RESTAURANT & LOUNGE ($$–$$$)

Easily Harvard Square's most sophisticated scene. Enjoy an oil-infused martini in the beautiful downstairs lounge (with a wall of water and Tibetan paintings) before heading upstairs for contemporary Asian-inspired cuisine.

B2 ⊠ 92 Winthrop Street

BRUNCH

Henrietta's Table ($$–$$$)
At The Charles Hotel (▷ 112). Awarded the "Best Brunch in Boston," other meals are equally inventive.

B2 ⊠ 1 Bennett Street
☎ 617/661-5005
⏰ Breakfast, brunch, lunch and dinner daily ⓠ Harvard

☎ 617/576-2800 ⏰ Lunch Mon–Sat, dinner daily, brunch Sun ⓠ Harvard

RIALTO ($$$)

www.rialto-restaurant.com
Star chef Jody Adams whips up a superb Mediterranean menu made from local ingredients and produce. More casual, but equally delicious, food is served in the restaurant's bar area.

A2 ⊠ The Charles Hotel, 1 Bennett Street ☎ 617/661-5050 ⏰ Dinner daily ⓠ Harvard

SANDRINE'S ($$$)

www.sandrines.com
Relaxed dining on Alsatian dishes worthy of full attention. Don't skip the salads (perhaps Cortland apples, blue cheese and spiced cashews) en route to the silky scallops or a *choucroute garnie* of meats and sausages cooked in Riesling.

A2 ⊠ 8 Holyoke Street ☎ 617/497-5300 ⏰ Lunch Mon–Sat, dinner daily ⓠ Harvard

UPSTAIRS ON THE SQUARE ($$–$$$)

www.upstairsonthesquare.com
Whimsical in its interior as much as in its cuisine, this elaborately appointed, multifloor restaurant excels at creations like Gruyère tart with Asian pear and black truffle.

B2 ⊠ 91 Winthrop Street ☎ 617/864-1933 ⏰ Lunch, dinner daily, afternoon tea Sat, brunch Sun ⓠ Harvard

You could easily spend weeks in Boston and not come to the end of all the city has to offer. Dozens of historical and cultural attractions lie within easy day-trip reach and are worth exploring in their own right.

Sights	102–104	Top 25	**TOP 25**
Excursions	105–106	Boston Harbor Islands ▷ **102**	
		JFK Library and Museum ▷ **103**	

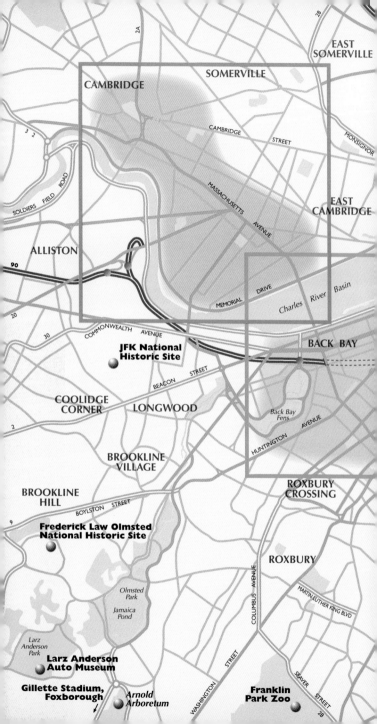

Mystic River

EAST
BOSTON

CHARLESTOWN

RUTHERFORD AVENUE

FATHER ADAMSKI MEMORIAL HIGHWAY

O'BRIEN HIGHWAY

JOHN FITZGERALD EXPRESSWAY

NORTH
END

WEST
END

BEACON
HILL

*Boston
Common*

FINANCIAL
DISTRICT

BOSTON

CHINATOWN

THEATER
DISTRICT

SOUTH
END

Boston Inner Harbor

*Boston
Harbor
Islands →*

SOUTH
BOSTON

COLUMBIA ROAD

MASSACHUSETTS AVENUE

GENERAL PULASKI SKYWAY

*Columbus
Park*

*Dorchester
Bay*

MORRISSEY BOULEVARD

SOUTHEAST EXPRESSWAY

**John F Kennedy
Library and Museum**

GROVE
HALL

SAVINHILL

| 0 | | 1 km |
| 0 | | 1 mile |

Farther Afield

Boston Harbor Islands

Peddocks Island in Boston Harbor

THE BASICS

www.bostonharborislands.org

www.nps.gov/boha/index.htm

🔳 Off map at M5

✉ Boston Harbor Islands, National Park Service, 408 Atlantic Avenue

☎ 617/223-8666

🕐 Georges Island: May to mid-Oct daily ferries. The other islands: May–Labor Day daily

🍴 Snack bar and barbecues on Georges. No drinking water on any islands. Take a picnic

🚢 Long Wharf, Quincy Shipyard and Logan Airport to Georges Island. Long Wharf and Quincy Shipyard to other islands. From Jun 1–Labor Day free water shuttles between islands

♿ Poor

💲 Ferry expensive. Water taxi free

❓ Organized activities and tours including lighthouse and occasional winter trips. Check websites for details

HIGHLIGHTS

- The sense of escape
- Picnicking on a beach
- Fort Warren's dungeons
- Views of Boston's skyline
- Bird-watching on all the islands

Gather wild raspberries, picnic on a beach, visit a ruined fort—all within sight of the city? These wildernesses are ringed by Boston, its airport and suburbs: It's just incredible they've escaped development.

National Recreation Area Once defensive sites and home to prisons and poorhouses, the Boston Harbor Islands were largely ignored until they became a National Recreation Area in 1996. People are beginning to appreciate these havens of wildlife, so near, yet so distant in feel.

Island hopping It's a 45-minute ferry ride from Long Wharf to Georges Island. From here water taxis loop to Lovells, Peddocks, Bumpkin and Grape. The islands are small, so you can visit more than one in a day; each has its own character. Georges attracts most visitors. All have picnic areas (there's no fresh water). Take guided walks, hike trails on your own or just beachcomb (beaches are mostly pebbly). Lovells has a sandy, supervised swimming beach.

Something for everyone On Georges clamber over Fort Warren (find the hidden spiral staircase and get superb views of the city). Peddocks and Lovells also have ruined forts. Bumpkin is where to pick raspberries. Join the hares on Lovells; study the wildlife in the rock pools, salt marsh and woodland on Peddocks; and on Grape, crunch along beaches covered in iridescent blue mussel shells.

"A man may die, nations may rise and fall, but an idea lives on," said the late president John F. Kennedy, whose life, leadership and legacy are brilliantly evoked in this dramatic museum by the sea.

The setting The presidential library and its museum, constructed in 1979, are housed in an I. M. Pei building on Dorchester Bay, 4 miles (6.5km) southeast of downtown Boston. The building's two towers, of dark glass and smooth white concrete, command fine views of the city, the bay and Boston Harbor Islands. The lawns, dune grass and wild roses on the grounds recall the Kennedy summer home on Cape Cod.

The New Museum An introductory film covers Kennedy's early years, from his childhood to the 1960 presidential campaign. Re-created settings include the White House corridors and the Oval Office, complete with the coconut inscribed "HELP" that led to his rescue after his naval ship sank in the Pacific. Videos cover significant events such as the Cuban Missile Crisis, space exploration and the assassination. Family photographs and exhibits cover the life and work of Jacqueline Kennedy Onassis.

The Presidential Library This is one of 13 presidential libraries holding the papers of 13 of the US presidents since Herbert Hoover. The Presidential Library System allows presidents to establish a library and museum.

THE BASICS

www.jfklibrary.org

✚ Off map at J9

✉ Columbia Point, Dorchester (Route 3/I-93 exit 15)

☎ 617/514-1600

🕐 Daily 9–5

🍴 Café on premises

🚇 JFK/U Mass then free shuttle bus

♿ Excellent

💵 Moderate. Boston CityPass applies

❓ Shop

HIGHLIGHTS

● The building, its setting and views
● Introductory video
● Oval Office
● Film and sound clips

TIP

● At the JFK Library, don't miss the Hemingway collection, which includes manuscripts and artifacts from the late, great writer.

More to see

ARNOLD ARBORETUM

Stunning in all seasons, this hilly park is part of the "Emerald Necklace."
✚ Off map at B9 ✉ 125 Arborway, Jamaica Plain ☎ 617/524-1718 ◉ Daily dawn–dusk ▣ Orange line to Forest Hills ▥ Free

FRANKLIN PARK ZOO

Wander through an African Tropical Forest, stroke small animals at the Children's Zoo, visit the lions, then picnic in the hills and meadows.
✚ Off map at G9 ✉ 1 Franklin Park Road ☎ 617/541-5466 ◉ Daily ▯ Café or picnic ▣ Forest Hills, then bus 16 ▥ Moderate

FREDERICK LAW OLMSTED NATIONAL HISTORIC SITE

The country's most famous landscape architect designed Boston Common, Central Park and the US Capitol grounds. At his workshop, visitors can tour the grounds and arrange weekend walking tours.
✚ Off map at A9 ✉ 99 Warren Street ☎ 617/566-1689 ◉ Reopening 2010 ▣ Brookline Hills (Green line D) then 0.75-mile (1.2km) walk ▥ Free

GILLETTE STADIUM

Gillette Stadium (an hour's drive south or train from South Station) is home to the New England Patriots (August–September) and the men's pro soccer team, New England Revolution (April–July).
✚ Off map at B9 ✉ Route 1, Foxborough ☎ 800/543-1776. Ticketmaster: 617/931-2000

JFK NATIONAL HISTORIC SITE

Take a trip to Camelot at President Kennedy's boyhood home, filled with photographs and other memorabilia.
✚ A7 ✉ 83 Beals Street ☎ 617/566-7937 ◉ May–Oct Wed–Sun 10–4.30 ▣ Coolidge Corner (Green line C) ▥ Tour inexpensive

LARZ ANDERSON AUTO MUSEUM

The world's largest private automobile collection—highlights include antique Mercedes and French cars.
✚ Off map at B9 ✉ 15 Newton Street, Brookline ☎ 617/522-6547 ◉ Tue–Sun 10–4 ▣ Cleveland Circle (Green line C), then bus 51 (not Sun) ▥ Inexpensive

Blazing fall color at the Arnold Arboretum

Excursions

PLYMOUTH

The Pilgrims left Plymouth, England, for the New World on the *Mayflower*. Their landing of 1620 (the exact location is debated) is commemorated on the waterfront by Plymouth Rock, the town having been named after the Devon port from where they set sail. Don't expect a boulder, however; most visitors are disappointed by the small size of the granite stone.

A more satisfying way to get in touch with the history of Massachusetts' first settlers is to visit them at Plimoth Plantation, a meticulously researched reproduction Pilgrim settlement 3 miles (5km) south. Here interpreters in period costume chat with visitors while getting on with their chores. The excellent curators work hard to make the village site accessible and display exhibits including how the Pilgrims' diet related to the seasons. At another exhibit, Hobbamock's Homesite, the Native Americans on whose ancestors' land the Pilgrims settled tell of their experiences. Also affiliated with the museum is the *Mayflower II*, a seaworthy replica of the ship that the Pilgrims sailed from England to the New World. Costumed interpreters provide below-decks tours and insight into the perilous crossing.

Plymouth is a popular destination and offers motels, restaurants and other attractions catering to visitors—some of them authentic, others tacky. One worth a stop is the Pilgrim Hall Museum, which is full of impressive artifacts once owned by the Pilgrims, including furniture, clothing and armor. While not quite as authentic, the Plymouth National Wax Museum will delight children, with key events in the history of the colony depicted in dioramas with life-size figures. One of the best times to visit Plymouth is during Thanksgiving, when the town pulls out all the stops with a parade and other events—and modern-day Native Americans stage an annual protest they call the "National Day of Mourning."

THE BASICS

www.visit-plymouth.com
Distance: 50 miles (80km)
Journey Time: 1 hour
☎ Plimoth Plantation: 508/746-1622
🕐 Plimoth Plantation and *Mayflower II*: late Mar–Nov
🚊 From South Station
💰 Plimoth Plantation, *Mayflower II*: expensive. Pilgrim Hall Museum: moderate
ℹ Destination Plymouth
✉ 170 Water Street, Suite 10c
☎ 508/747-7533

HIGHLIGHTS

- Plimoth Plantation
- Hobbamock's Homesite
- The *Mayflower II*
- Plymouth Rock
- Pilgrim Hall Museum

THE BASICS

Concord
www.concordchamberof
commerce.org
Distance: 20 miles (32km)
Journey Time: 40 minutes
🕐 Emerson's and
Hawthorne's houses closed
winter; other sites open all
year. Hours vary
🚂 From North Station
ℹ️ Concord Chamber of
Commerce
✉️ 58 Main Street
☎ 978/369-3120

THE BASICS

Salem
www.salem.org
Distance: 16 miles (26km)
Journey Time: 30 minutes
🕐 Peabody Essex
Museum: Tue–Sun, hol Mon
10–5. Witch Museum: daily
🚂 From North Station
🚢 From Long Wharf
🏛️ Peabody Essex
Museum: expensive. Witch
Museum: moderate
ℹ️ Destination Salem
✉️ 63 Wharf Street
☎ 978/744-3663

*From left: Captain Parker
statue in Lexington; bandstand; Roger Conant statue;
House of the Seven Gables in
Salem; Witch Museum sign*

LEXINGTON AND CONCORD

**These lovely towns are immortalized by
events that sparked the first shots of
the Revolution.**

It was to Lexington, where Patriot leaders were
staying, that Paul Revere made his famous ride to
warn of British plans to seize a cache of arms in
Concord. It was on Concord's North Bridge, on
April 19, 1775, that the "shot heard round the
world" was fired. Concord has a literary past, too,
as the home of influential early 19th-century
writers and thinkers Henry David Thoreau,
Ralph Waldo Emerson, Nathaniel Hawthorne and
Louisa May Alcott. Visit their houses, and their
graves in Sleepy Hollow Cemetery.

SALEM

**To many, Salem means witches, so it's
not surprising to find a range of interpre-
tations of the mass hysteria that hit the
town in the 1690s.**

The most popular attraction is the Salem Witch
Museum, which treads a fine line between cheap
thrills and historical accuracy in telling the macabre
tale of the trials that claimed 19 lives. Other sites
worth visiting are the Witch House, which
belonged to the presiding judge, and the affecting
memorial to the victims on Salem Common.

Less well known but far more striking once
you're there is that the town also has a rich
maritime history and some of the best Federal
architecture in America. In the 18th and early 19th
centuries Salem's prosperous shipbuilders,
merchants and sea captains built graceful houses
and filled them with beautiful things. Many of
these objects are in the Peabody Essex Museum.

The places to rest your head around Boston run from family-run bed-and-breakfasts to elaborate, world-class hotels. The majority are a convenient walking distance from the major sights.

Introduction	108
Budget Hotels	109
Mid-Range Hotels	110–111
Luxury Hotels	112

Where to Stay

Introduction

Boston has no shortage of places to stay, all to suit your personal preferences for style, noise level, amenities and location.

Bed-and-Breakfasts and Inns

Bed-and-breakfasts are often run out of a private home. They normally include a modest bedroom, plus a home-cooked breakfast, at a reasonable price. Boston and Cambridge have a number of such establishments in the city. A bit more luxurious and larger than a bed-and-breakfast, the best inns around Boston are often housed in historic buildings or town houses. They also often include breakfast, though sometimes charge a separate fee. Some have such modern amenities as flat-screen televisions, CD players and whirlpool tubs.

Boutique and Luxury Hotels

Over the last several years, a stable of chic, modern small hotels has cropped up. The majority offer stylish, contemporary design, hip restaurants on the property and concierge services. They are mostly in and around downtown Boston. Scattered throughout Boston's most popular neighborhoods (from Back Bay and Downtown to Harvard Square), the area's luxury hotels cater to the traveler's every need and whim. Some offer quirky amenities (authors library in the lobby at Harvard Square's Charles Hotel) alongside services such as in-room massages and personal shoppers.

HISTORIC HOTELS

A handful of the city's most history-laden sites are also places you can stay the night. The **Omni Parker House** (▷ 111) is America's longest continuously operating luxury hotel. Opened in 1855, it was the meeting site of a literary group that included Ralph Waldo Emerson and Nathaniel Hawthorne. Later, its dining room gained a place in Boston history as the site of President (then Senator) John F. Kennedy's proposal to Jacqueline Bouvier. The **Fairmont Copley Plaza** (▷ 112) has witnessed many of Boston's grandest celebrations.

The Lenox Hotel is a boutique hotel in the Back Bay (top)

Budget Hotels

Expect to pay between $75 and $150 per night for a budget hotel.

BERKELEY RESIDENCE YWCA
www.ywcaboston.org
Located in Boston's South End, this pleasant hotel and residence offers basic single, double and dorm-style rooms with shared bathrooms for reasonable prices. Full breakfast is included, and there is a TV Room.
✚ H7 ✉ 40 Berkeley Street ☎ 617/375-2524 🚇 Back Bay Station

BEST WESTERN
www.bestwestern.com
Located less than a mile from Fenway Park and the Museum of Fine Arts.

OUT OF TOWN

To reduce hotel costs, consider staying in Concord, Salem or Rockport, all 40–60 minutes from Boston and served by regular train services. Contact:
Concord Chamber of Commerce
☎ 978/369-3120; www.concordchamberof commerce.org
Destination Salem
☎ 978/744-3663; www.salem.org
Rockport Chamber of Commerce ☎ 978/546-6575; www.rockportusa.com

✚ D9 ✉ 342 Longwood Avenue ☎ 617/731-4700 or 800/468-2378; fax 617/731-4870 🚇 Green line D to Longwood

CHANDLER INN
www.chandlerinn.com
Basic 56-room hotel in the attractive South End. Gay-friendly. Short walk to Tremont Street restaurant row and Copley Square.
✚ H7 ✉ 26 Chandler Street ☎ 617/482-3450 or 800/ 842-3450; fax 617/542-3428 🚇 Back Bay Station

COLLEGE CLUB
www.thecollegeclubofboston. com
You don't have to be a student to book one of the attractive single rooms here. Some rooms have shared bathrooms.
✚ G6 ✉ 44 Commonwealth Avenue ☎ 617/536-9510; fax 617/247-8537 🚇 Arlington

COMFORT INN
www.choicehotels.com
Inexpensive option 3 miles (5km) south of town. Outdoor pool, bowling alley nearby. 133 rooms.
✚ Off map at K9 ✉ 900 Morrissey Boulevard, Dorchester ☎ 617/287-9200; fax 617/282-2365 🚇 JFK/U Mass, then half-hourly hotel shuttle bus 7am–10pm

HI-BOSTON
www.hiusa.org
Hostelling International USA offers dormitories; cooking facilities available. 205 beds.
✚ E8 ✉ 12 Hemenway

Street, Back Bay ☎ 617/536-9455; fax 617/424-6558 🚇 Hynes Convention Center

JOHN JEFFRIES HOUSE
www.johnjeffrieshouse.com
Four-floor brick inn on Beacon Hill; 46 tiny rooms. The two-room suites are better value.
✚ H5 ✉ 14 David Mugar Way (formerly Embankment Road) at Charles Circle ☎ 617/367-1866; fax 617/ 742-0313 🚇 Charles/MGH

NEWBURY GUEST HOUSE
www.newburyguesthouse.com
Victorian-style rooms—32 in all—in three connected redbrick row houses. Excellent value, popular; reserve well ahead.
✚ G6 ✉ 261 Newbury Street, Back Bay ☎ 617/ 437-7666 or 800/437-7668; fax 617/670-6100 🚇 Copley, Hynes Convention Center

BED-AND-BREAKFAST

Double occupancy in bed-and-breakfast accommodation ranges from $90 to $180. Try the **Bed-and-Breakfast Agency of Boston**, a helpful, friendly agency that will find you accommodation in historic houses and restored waterfront lofts. Nightly, weekly, monthly and winter rates (✉ 47 Commercial Wharf ☎ 617/ 720-3540, 800/248-9262 or 0800 895 128 from the UK; fax 617/523-5761; www. boston-bnbagency. com).

Mid-Range Hotels

WHERE TO STAY | MID-RANGE HOTELS

PRICES

Expect to pay between $150 and $275 per night for a mid-range hotel.

BACK BAY HILTON
www.hilton.com
Convenient to the Pru and Hynes centers. 390 rooms.
✚ F7 ✉ 40 Dalton Street, Back Bay ☎ 617/236-1100 or 800/874-0663; fax 617/867-6104 Ⓜ Prudential, Hynes Convention Center

BEACON HILL HOTEL AND BISTRO
www.beaconhillhotel.com
Thirteen tasteful, unfussy rooms in two linked townhouses. Lovely roof deck.
✚ H5 ✉ 25 Charles Street ☎ 617/723-7575 or 888/959-2442; fax 617/723-7525 Ⓜ Charles/MGH

BOSTON PARK PLAZA
www.bostonparkplaza.com
Elegant hotel built in 1927, with 950 rooms. Near the Public Garden and Theater District. Family friendly.
✚ H6 ✉ 64 Arlington Street ☎ 617/426-2000 or 800/225-2008; fax 617/426-5545 Ⓜ Arlington

LA CAPELLA SUITES
www.lacappellasuites.com
Bare-bones B&B accommodations in the North End give you enviable access to the restaurants and cafés of Hanover Street.
✚ K4 ✉ 290 North Street ☎ 617/523-9020 Ⓜ Haymarket

COLONNADE
www.colonnadehotel.com
Behind the bland 1960s facade of this 285-room hotel near the Pru are traditionally decorated rooms. Rooftop pool. Home of Brasserie Jo.
✚ F7 ✉ 120 Huntington Avenue, Back Bay ☎ 617/424-7000 or 800/962-3030; fax 617/424-1717 Ⓜ Prudential

CONSTITUTION INN
www.constitution.com
Within sight of its namesake ship, this spartan, nautically themed inn offers military discounts.
✚ K2 ✉ 150 3rd Avenue, Charlestown ☎ 617/241-8400 Ⓜ North Station

MORE OPTIONS

Hyatt Regency, Cambridge
www.cambridge.hyatt.com
On the Charles River, with a revolving rooftop lounge. 469 rooms.
✉ 575 Memorial Drive ☎ 617/492-1234 or 800/233-1234; fax 617/491-6906 Ⓜ Kendall

A Cambridge House
www.acambridgehouse.com
A Victorian bed-and-breakfast inn in north Cambridge. 15 rooms.
✉ 2218 Massachusetts Avenue ☎ 617/491-6300 or 800/232-9989; fax 617/868-2848 Ⓜ Davis, Porter

COURTYARD BOSTON TREMONT HOTEL
www.marriott.com
In the heart of the Theater District, this branch of the Marriott Courtyard chain inhabits an historic 1925 building.
✚ J6 ✉ 275 Tremont Street ☎ 617/426-1400; fax 617/482-6730 Ⓜ Boylston

ELIOT
www.eliothotel.com
Elegance, comfort and value. 95 rooms and suites with living room and kitchenette.
✚ E6 ✉ 370 Commonwealth Avenue, Back Bay ☎ 617/267-1607 or 800/44 ELIOT; fax 617/536-9114 Ⓜ Hynes Convention Center

GRYPHON HOUSE
www.inboston.com
Each of the eight rooms at this well-appointed B&B has its own distinct identity. Around the corner from Fenway Park.
✚ E6 ✉ 9 Bay State Road ☎ 617/375-9003 Ⓜ Kenmore

HAMPTON INN & SUITES BOSTON CROSSTOWN CENTER
www.bostonhamptoninn.com
Good value at this modern-feeling hotel on the edge of the South End. Free shuttle to many city attractions.
✚ F7 ✉ 811 Massachusetts Avenue ☎ 617/445-6400 Ⓜ Massachusetts Avenue (Orange line)

HARBORSIDE INN

www.harborsideinnboston.com

A can't-beat downtown location and elegant furnishings make this independent hotel good value for the money.

K5 ⊠ 185 State Street ☎ 617/723-7500; fax 617/670-6015 🚇 State

HOTEL MARLOWE

www.hotelmarlowe.com

Overlooking the Charles River near the Science Museum, this elegant hotel is big and boutique at the same time. Rooms are lushly decorated and service is far beyond the price range.

H3 ⊠ 24 Edwin Land Boulevard ☎ 617/868-8000 or 800/825-7140 🚇 Lechmere

HYATT REGENCY BOSTON

www.regencyboston.hyatt.com

Opened in late 2004, this 22-floor, 500-room hotel is close to Faneuil Hall and the Theater District.

J6 ⊠ One Avenue de Lafayette ☎ 617/912-1234 or 800/492-8804; fax 617/451-2198 🚇 Downtown Crossing

INN AT HARVARD

www.theinnatharvard.com

Luxurious accommodations characterize this plush hotel affiliated with Harvard University.

B2 ⊠ 1201 Massachusetts Avenue, Cambridge ☎ 617/491-2222 🚇 Harvard

JEWEL OF NEWBURY

www.jewelboston.com

Take an exotic vacation-within-a-vacation with the eye-popping array of antiques from around the world at this intimate Back Bay B&B.

F7 ⊠ 254 Newbury Street ☎ 617/536-5523 🚇 Hynes Convention Center

KENDALL HOTEL

www.kendallhotel.com

A former firehouse close to MIT and just over the bridge to Boston has been converted into a comfortable boutique hotel, complete with Americana furnishings.

F4 ⊠ 350 Main Street,

SOUTH END B&BS

Herbst Haus
www.herbsthaus.com
A Victorian town house in the South End with two comfortable suites.
⊠ Appleton Street
☎ 617/266-0235
🚇 Back Bay Station

The Copley Inn
www.copleyinn.com
The classic brick row house has 20 double rooms, each with kitchenette and bath. There's no front desk and no elevator, but the homey atmosphere and central location make it popular.
F7 ⊠ 19 Garrison Street
☎ 617/236-0300
🚇 Prudential

Cambridge ☎ 866/566-1300 🚇 Kendall

MARY PRENTISS INN

www.maryprentissinn.com

A 20-room, antiques-filled bed-and-breakfast with modern amenities.

E9 ⊠ 6 Prentiss Street ☎ 617/661-2929; fax 617/661-5989 🚇 Porter

OMNI PARKER HOUSE

www.omnihotels.com

A rather staid 551-room, 19th-century hotel, near Boston Common. The Parker House roll and Boston cream pie were invented here.

J5 ⊠ 60 School Street, Downtown ☎ 617/227-8600 or 800/843-6664; fax 617/742-5729 🚇 Park Street

RADISSON HOTEL

www.radisson.com/bostonma

The Radisson has a convenient Theater District location plus a fitness club, pool and rooftop sundeck overlooking the city.

J6 ⊠ 200 Stuart Street ☎ 617/482-1800 🚇 Boylston

SHERATON BOSTON

www.starwood.com/sheraton

1,215 rooms in two 29-floor towers, connected by interior walkways to the Pru and Hynes. Caters to business travelers, but is also family-friendly.

G7 ⊠ Prudential Center, 39 Dalton Street ☎ 617/236-2000 or 800/325-3535; fax 617/236–1702 🚇 Prudential, Hynes Convention Center

Luxury Hotels

PRICES

Expect to pay more than $275 per night for a luxury hotel.

BOSTON HARBOR
www.bhh.com
Modern, elegant, 230-room hotel on the waterfront. It's worth paying a little more for harbor views. Good restaurant, with views.
L5 70 Rowes Wharf 617/439-7000 or 800/752-7077; fax 617/330-9450 Aquarium

THE CHARLES HOTEL
www.charleshotel.com
Modern 293-room hotel in Harvard Square. Home to Henrietta's Table (panel, ▷ 98) and Regattabar (▷ 97).
B2 1 Bennett Street, Cambridge 617/864-1200 or 800/882-1818; fax 617/864-5715 Harvard

COPLEY SQUARE
www.copleysquarehotel.com
143-room hotel with European flavor. Fitness facility and Xhale restaurant.
G6 47 Huntington Avenue, Back Bay 617/536-9000 or 800/225-7062; fax 617/421-1402 Copley

FAIRMONT COPLEY PLAZA
www.fairmont.com
A "grand dame" of Boston, with sumptuous decor. 383 rooms.
G6 138 St. James Avenue, Back Bay 617/267-5300 or 866/540-4417; fax 617/267-7668 Copley

FOUR SEASONS
www.fourseasons.com/boston
Top-notch elegance and service. Fine dining in the Bristol Lounge (▷ 61). 272 rooms.
H6 200 Boylston Street, Back Bay 617/338-4400 or 800/332-3442; fax 617/423-0154 Arlington

LANGHAM HOTEL
www.langhamhotels.com
Historic 1920s building with luxurious comforts. 326 rooms. Café Fleuri restaurant (▷ 61).
K5 250 Franklin Street 617/451-1900; fax 617/423-2844 State, Downtown Crossing

LENOX
www.lenoxhotel.com
Built in 1900, this 212-room independent is one of the best.
G6 710 Boylston Street 617/536-5300 or 800/225-7676; fax 617/267-1237 Copley

THE LIBERTY HOTEL
www.libertyhotel.com
Brilliant transformation of a grim old city jail into a stunning contemporary hotel with river views. There's just enough tongue-in-cheek reference to its past to be fun.
H4 215 Charles Street 617/224-4000 or 866/507-5245 Charles/MGH

W HOTEL BOSTON

Dramatic, contemporary and sophisticated. Rooms are high-tech, chic and modern with 235 rooms on 28 floors.
J6 100 Stuart Street 617/261-8700; fax 617/261-8725 Boylston

MILLENNIUM BOSTONIAN
www.millenniumhotels.com
This 201-room hotel is more intimate than some, and offers comfort without glitz. North 26 Restaurant.
K5 Faneuil Hall Marketplace 617/523-3600 or 866/866-8086; fax 617/523–2454 State, Government Center

NINE ZERO
www.ninezero.com
When the stars are in town, they stay at this chic boutique hotel on the Freedom Trail. Rooms are tricked out with all the latest gadgets and amenities.
J6 90 Tremont Street 617/772-5800; fax 617/772-5810 Park Street

SEAPORT HOTEL
www.seaportboston.com
In Boston's newest downtown neighborhood, the hotel is opposite the World Trade Center and the new Institute of Contemporary Art. It's a class act, with fine dining at Aura, a full spa, in-room wireless and interactive web portal.
M6 1 Seaport Lane (Northern Avenue) 617/385-4000 or 800/440-3318 World Trade Center

Need to Know

This section contains practical information about getting to Boston and traveling around once you are there, as well as tips, useful phone numbers, money matters and public holidays.

Planning Ahead   114–115

Getting There   116–117

Getting Around   118–119

Essential Facts   120–123

Timeline   124–125

Planning Ahead

When to Go

Summer and fall are peak visiting seasons. Hotels are busy at graduation time (May, June) and rates go up. In October you will get a glimpse of New England's fall foliage (better still farther north). The time between Thanksgiving and New Year is full of seasonal festivities.

AVERAGE DAILY MAXIMUM TEMPERATURES											
JAN	FEB	MAR	APR	MAY	JUN	JUL	AUG	SEP	OCT	NOV	DEC
37°F	37°F	46°F	56°F	66°F	76°F	82°F	80°F	75°F	63°F	52°F	37°F
3°C	3°C	8°C	13°C	19°C	24°C	28°C	26°C	24°C	17°C	11°C	3°C

Spring (April through May) is unpredictable, but can be wonderful, with cool nights and fresh days. This is when you can catch the magnolia blossoms in the Back Bay.

Summer (June through August) is normally pleasantly warm, but occasional heatwaves can see temperatures soaring into the 90s.

Fall (September through November) is warm in September and crisp in October and November, when the foliage is at its most colorful.

Winter (December through March) is very cold. Even when the sky is blue winds can be biting. Snows occasionally transform the city; a slushy, gray mess inevitably follows.

WHAT'S ON

January *Martin Luther King* weekend.

February *Chinese New Year* (Jan/Feb).

March *Spring Flower Show.* *St. Patrick's Day Parade.*

April *Patriots' Day* (3rd Mon): Revere's Ride is re-created.

Boston Marathon (3rd Mon).

Kite Festival (or May): held in Franklin Park.

May *May Fair* in Harvard Square.

Boston Pops Concerts.

June *Battle of Bunker Hill:* re-enactment (Sun before Bunker Hill Day, Jun 17).

Boston Globe Jazz Festival.

July *Boston Pops Concerts.* Independence celebrations (week of Jul 4): Boston Pops concert with fireworks, Boston Harborfest music festival and USS *Constitution* turnaround.

Italian feste (festivals, Jul/Aug weekends): North End.

August *Moon Festival:* Colorful processions in Chinatown.

September *Cambridge River Festival:* Events on the river.

Boston Arts Festival: Columbus Waterfront.

Boston Symphony Orchestra: Season Sep–May.

October *Columbus Day Parade.*

Head of the Charles Regatta (3rd week).

November *Christmas tree lighting ceremonies:* Faneuil Hall Marketplace and Charles Square, Cambridge.

Boston Ballet—The Nutcracker (Nov–Dec): Wang Center.

December *Tree lighting ceremonies:* Prudential Center, Harvard Square.

Boston Tea Party (mid-Dec): Re-enactment.

Carol concert: Trinity Church.

Boston Online

www.boston.com
The *Boston Globe*'s website has the daily newspaper, with local news, listings and restaurant reviews.

www.boston.citysearch.com
A guide to local events, theater productions, movies, concerts, sports, stores and restaurants. The site tends to feature big-name destinations and happenings, so you'll find everything from top-10 restaurant lists and heavy-hitter museum exhibits to addresses, phone numbers, schedules and maps.

www.bostonphoenix.com
The *Boston Phoenix* is a weekly alternative newspaper that offers detailed arts and entertainment listings, plus restaurant reviews.

www.bostonusa.com
Run by the Greater Boston Convention and Visitors Bureau, this site includes details about attractions, events, hotels and the subway, as well as other useful visitor information.

www.cambridge-usa.org
This is the Cambridge Office for Tourism's site and it contains listings of hotels, restaurants, attractions and arts and entertainment venues, as well as an events calendar and general visitor information for the City of Cambridge.

www.dailycandy.com
Click onto the Boston edition of this national site to find listings for the city's brand new restaurants and hottest stores, eclectic shows and services and other undiscovered gems.

www.mbta.com
The website of the MBTA (Massachusetts Bay Transportation Authority) is the place to look for timetables, maps and fare information for the T (subway), as well as buses and commuter rail services.

PRIME TRAVEL SITES

www.fodors.com
A complete travel-planning site. You can research prices and weather; book air tickets, cars and rooms; ask questions (and get answers) from fellow travelers; and find links to other sites.

www.massvacation.com
Visitor information from the Massachusetts Office of Travel and Tourism. The site includes an accommodation booking service.

www.orbitz.com
An air-fare search engine owned by five US airlines. It frequently offers low-fare specials.

www.discovernewengland. org
This is the official site for the states of New England, if you are planning a visit beyond Boston.

INTERNET CAFÉ

FedEx Kinko's
Copy and printing shops that offer internet access. Locations include:

✚ F5 ✉ 187 Dartmouth Street (Back Bay) ☎ 617/262-6188 🕐 24 hours 🚇 Back Bay Station, Copley 💵 $15 per hour

✚ C2 ✉ Mifflin Place (off Mt. Auburn Street, Harvard Square) ☎ 617/497-0125 🕐 24 hours 🚇 Harvard 💵 $15 per hour

Getting There

ENTRY REQUIREMENTS

Visitors to the US must show a full passport, valid for at least six months. Visitors using the Visa Waiver Program must register their details online before traveling. Regulations can change, so always check before you travel (☎ 202/643-4000; www.usembassy.gov). Leave plenty of time for clearing security and check the latest advice beforehand.

CAR RENTAL

Logan Airport has eight car rental companies operating within it; reserve in advance.

Alamo
www.goalamo.com
☎ 800/327-9633

Avis
www.avis.com
☎ 800/831-2847

Budget
www.budget.com
☎ 800/527-0700

Dollar
www.dollar.com
☎ 800/800-4000

Enterprise
www.enterprise.com
☎ 800/325-8007

Hertz
www.hertz.com
☎ 800/654-3131

National
www.nationalcar.com
☎ 800/227-7368

Thrifty
www.thrifty.com
☎ 800/367-2277

AIRPORTS

Logan Airport is on an island in Boston Harbor. It has four terminals, hotels and restaurants. Domestic flights also use T. F. Green Airport (Rhode Island), Manchester Airport (New Hampshire) and Worcester Airport (Massachusetts).

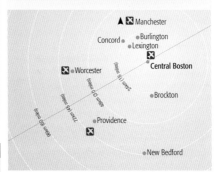

FROM LOGAN AIRPORT

For general airport information ☎ 800/235-6426. "Massport Shuttle" buses run every 20 minutes (5.30am–1am; free) from every terminal to Airport subway (T) station; from here it's a few minutes' journey to central Boston ($2).

Taxis cost $20–$30 (including a tunnel toll, but not tip). Thanks to the new Massachusetts Turnpike extensions from Logan, travel time to and from the airport has been reduced dramatically. Allow roughly 15 minutes to or from Back Bay (▷ panel, opposite).

Harbor Express (☎ 617/222-6999) is an exciting way to arrive in central Boston. It's a 10-minute boat ride between Logan and Long Wharf in the Financial District, where you can pick up a taxi. Harbor Express also operates between Logan and Quincy and Hull, on the south shore (Mon–Fri 5.55am–11pm, Sat 8am–10pm, Sun 8am–9pm; $10 to Long Wharf). An on-call City Water Taxi (☎ 617/422-0392) runs all year from Logan to 20 different waterfront locations (Mon–Sat 7am–10pm, Sun 7am–8pm; $10). Shuttle buses connect all terminals with the water taxis.

OTHER AIRPORTS

Domestic flights also use T. F. Green Airport, Rhode Island (☎ 401/737-8222); Manchester Airport, New Hampshire (☎ 603/624-6539); and Worcester Airport, Massachusetts (☎ 508/799-1741). It's then more than an hour's bus ride to Boston.

ARRIVING BY BUS

Greyhound (☎ 800/231-2222) and Peter Pan Trailways (☎ 800/343-9999) travel between New York and Boston's South Station, and (less frequently) to the rest of the USA and Canada.

ARRIVING BY CAR

Boston can be a difficult city to drive in for visitors, and parking is scarce. The Big Dig highway construction project, which reorganized highways into and through Boston, is now complete. If you do drive, select a hotel with free parking, get a good map and plan your route. The major east-west highway into Boston is the I-90 toll road, also known as the Massachusetts Turnpike. I-90 links up with I-93 just south of downtown. I-93 is the major north-south highway, and it travels through tunnels under downtown Boston. I-95, the East Coast's major north-south interstate highway, circles the perimeter of the Boston metropolitan area.

ARRIVING BY TRAIN

Amtrak (☎ 800/872-7245; www.amtrak.com) runs a frequent service between Boston's South Station and Providence, New York, Philadelphia and Washington, D.C. The high-speed Acela service between New York and Boston takes three and a half hours. South Station also serves Washington, D.C. and Chicago. Amtrak's Down-easter travels up the coast to Maine from North Station. Trains running in New England tend to arrive and depart on time, but those traveling longer distances are frequently delayed—particularly in winter, when snow slows them down—usually anywhere from 10 minutes to an hour.

TIME TO LOGAN

From downtown Boston, driving to Logan averages 15 minutes. However, during heavy traffic hours (generally 7.30–9.30am and 4.30–6pm on weekdays), count on the ride taking 30 minutes, possibly even 40 in the dead of rush hour. Security lines on international flights can also be quite long, so plan accordingly.

EATING ON THE RUN

At Logan Airport, find:
Legal Sea Foods (where you can also buy live lobsters to package up and take home with you).
Wolfgang Puck, quick and healthy pizzas.
Houlihan's, homemade soups and sandwiches to steaks, ribs and seafood.
Boston Beer Works, micro-brews and American food.
Johnny Rockets, American burgers, shakes and jukebox.
Fresh City, wrap sandwiches to go.
Starbucks, for fresh-ground coffee, lattes and sandwiches.

In South Station, find:
Rosie's Bakery, for rich fudges, cakes and brownies.
Au Bon Pain, sandwiches, soups and salads.
Pizzeria Regina, locally loved, small Italian chain.
Surf City Squeeze, for fresh-made fruit smoothies.

Getting Around

BICYCLES

Boston is now attempting to become a bicycle-friendly town. Meanwhile, if you are looking to get some exercise outside the city, Boston has several bicycle paths that offer pleasant riding. One is the Southwest Corridor, which runs from behind the Massachusetts Avenue T stop all the way out to the Arnold Arboretum in Jamaica Plain. A longer ride is the Minuteman Bikeway, which runs from Davis Square in Somerville all the way out to Bedford–passing the historical sites in Lexington (▷ 106) on the way.

VISITORS WITH DISABILITIES

An Airport Handicap Van offers a free service between all Logan Airport locations. Use the free "Van Phone" in the baggage-claim area. Public buildings, parking areas and most subway stations provide wheelchair access, and many hotels have specially designed rooms. Modern or newly renovated hotels and restaurants tend to be better equipped. For further information contact: New England INDEX ✉ 200 Trapelo Road, Waltham, MA 02452 ☎ 781/642-0248; www.disabilityinfo.org

VISITOR PASSES

● An MBTA (Massachusetts Bay Transportation Authority) Link Pass gives unlimited travel for one or seven days ($9, $15) on all subways, buses and ferries. It is available at vending machines in T stations and online in advance at www.mbta.com. They are NOT available at visitor information centers.

BOATS

● MBTA ferry/Boston Harbor cruises (☎ 617/227-4321) link Long Wharf and Charlestown, Long Wharf and Provincetown.

BUSES

● Buses travel farther out into the suburbs than the T, but the T is much quicker and easier in the center.
● Passengers must have the exact change ($1.50) or Charlie Card. Express Bus has an additional charge.
● For travel farther afield, bus companies operate out of South Station serving destinations throughout New England.

SUBWAY (T)

● Boston's system of subway and elevated trains is known as the T. The five lines—Red, Green, Orange, Silver and Blue—meet in central Boston. "Inbound" and "Outbound" refer to direction in relation to Park Street Station.
● The clean and efficient trains run from 5am (later on Sunday) to 12.45am.
● Rides are now by Charlie Cards, reloadable cards bought at vending machines in stations. Individual rides are $1.70 or $2, depending on the plan selected. These machines are not especially easy for the first-time user, so it is a good idea to visit www.mbta.com in advance, for a clear explanation of the options and operation of machines.
● Free maps are available at the Park Street Station information booth. Note that some maps do not show all stops on the Green line branches.

TAXIS

● Hail taxis on the street or find them at hotels and taxi stands.
● 24-hour taxi services include:
Yellow Cab ☎ 617/547-3000
Metrocab Cab ☎ 617/782-5500
Town Taxis ☎ 617/536-5000

TRAINS

● MBTA commuter trains leave from North Station for destinations west and north, including Lowell, Concord, Salem, Manchester, Gloucester, Rockport and Ipswich. South Station serves Plymouth and Providence.

DRIVING AND CAR RENTAL
Car rental

● Rental drivers must be at least 21; many companies put the minimum age at 25 or charge extra for those between 21 and 25.
● For car rental companies, ▷ 116.
● Consider using the subway to pick up your car from a rental agency on the outskirts of Boston to avoid having to drive in the city.

Driving

● Driving and parking in Boston is challenging.
● Park only in legal spots, or you will be towed. Park in the direction of the traffic.
● Speed limits on the major highways range from 55 to 65mph (90 to 104kph); elsewhere they range from 30 to 45mph (48 to 72kph).
● All front seat passengers must wear a seat belt. Children under 12 years old must sit in the back and use an approved car seat or safety belt.
● You may turn right at a red traffic light if the road ahead is clear, unless signage prohibits it.
● Drink/driving laws are strict. Never drive after drinking; don't keep opened alcohol in the car.
● Look out for one-way streets, especially in downtown Boston where they are legion. Boston taxi drivers are aggressive—the best defense is to yield whenever necessary. And don't be afraid to use your horn!

PEDICABS

A fun and efficient alternative to taxis and subways are the "cycle rickshaws" run by Boston Pedicabs (617/266-2005; www.bostonpedicab.com). The bicycle cabs are easy to find Downtown and can take you to where you are going quickly.

TAXI FARES

At the time of publication, taxi rates are $2.60 for the first 1/7 mile (0.23km), and $0.40 for each additional 1/7 mile (0.23km); or $28 for each hour spent waiting. (Be sure to check rates at the airport.) Trips to and from the airport are subject to additional tolls of $2.75 and $8, respectively; there is no charge for luggage. For trips beyond 12 miles (20km) from downtown Boston, a flat-rate applies: www.cityofboston.gov

Essential Facts

TRAVEL INSURANCE

It is vital to have cover for medical expenses, as well as for theft, baggage loss, trip cancellation and accidents. Check your insurance coverage and buy a supplementary policy as needed.

MONEY

The currency is the dollar (=100 cents). Notes (bills) are in denominations of $1, $5, $10, $20, $50 and $100; coins are 25¢ (a quarter), 10¢ (a dime), 5¢ (a nickel) and 1¢ (a penny). You may find that small businesses will not break a $100, $50 or even $20 bill.

5 dollars

10 dollars

50 dollars

100 dollars

ALCOHOL

● It is illegal to drink alcohol in public places such as the T. Do not keep opened bottles of alcohol in the car.

● It is illegal to sell alcohol to anyone under the age of 21. Alcohol is not sold in shops on Sunday or after 11pm Monday through Saturday.

MAGAZINES AND NEWSPAPERS

● Free tourist magazines are found in hotel lobbies, and include discount coupons.

● Listings can be found in the *Boston Globe* (Thursday), the *Boston Herald* (Friday) and the *Boston Phoenix* (Thursday; free).

● *Boston Magazine* (monthly) reviews the Boston scene and gives awards to restaurants.

MAIL

● Letter boxes are gray/blue and have swing-top lids. Most hotels will mail letters for you.

MONEY MATTERS

● Nearly all banks have Automatic Teller Machines. Cards registered in other countries that are linked to the Cirrus or Plus networks are accepted. Before leaving, check which network your cards are linked to and ensure your PIN is valid in the US, where four-figure numbers are the norm.

● Credit cards are widely accepted.

● US dollar traveler's checks function like cash in larger hotels and stores.

● Money and traveler's checks can be exchanged at most banks (check fees as they can be high) and many travel centers in central Boston.

● Some businesses may ask for photo identification before cashing traveler's checks.

OPENING HOURS

● Banks: Mon–Fri 9–4, Thu 9–5 or later, Sat 9–12.

● Shops: Mon–Sat 10–6 or later. Closed Sun mornings.

• Museums and sights: Unless otherwise stated, all sights mentioned in this book close on Thanksgiving and Christmas.
• Businesses: Mon–Fri 8 or 9–5.

PUBLIC HOLIDAYS
• **Jan 1** (New Year's Day)
• **3rd Mon in Jan** (Martin Luther King Day)
• **3rd Mon in Feb** (President's Day)
• **Last Mon in May** (Memorial Day)
• **July 4** (Independence Day)
• **1st Mon in Sep** (Labor Day)
• **2nd Mon in Oct** (Columbus Day)
• **Nov 11** (Veterans Day)
• **4th Thu in Nov** (Thanksgiving)
• **Dec 25** (Christmas Day)
• Boston also celebrates: **Mar 17** (Evacuation Day); **3rd Mon in Apr** (Patriots' Day); **Jun 17** (Bunker Hill Day).

SENSIBLE PRECAUTIONS
• Boston is basically a safe city, but it is wise to stick to well-lit and well-populated areas after dark. Avoid the lower half of Washington Street and Boston Common at night.
• Discuss your itinerary with your hotel's reception staff so they can point out any potential problems.
• Be aware of the people around you, especially at night or in quiet areas.
• Keep your wallet or purse out of sight and don't carry valuables or cash openly. Do not carry easily snatched bags and cameras, or put your wallet into your back pocket.
• Keep valuables in your hotel's safe and never carry more money than you need.
• Lost traveler's checks are relatively quick and easy to replace. Keep the numbers of the checks separate from the checks themselves.
• Report any stolen item to the nearest police station, if only to be able to claim on your insurance. The police will fill out the forms your insurance company will need.
• Always lock car doors and keep valuables out of sight.

SMOKING
• Smoking is banned in restaurants unless there is a separate seating area. It is banned in many public places, including the T. Some hotels have no-smoking floors.
• Cambridge is by law smoke-free.

LOST AND FOUND

● To report lost credit cards:
American Express
☎ 800/528-2121;
Diners Club/Carte Blanche
☎ 800/234-6377;
MasterCard
☎ 800/826-2181;
Visa ☎ 800/227-6811
● Lost traveler's checks:
American Express
☎ 800/221-7282;
Thomas Cook
☎ 800/732-1322

PARKING

If you plan on driving in
Boston, note that the city is
notorious for its lack of parking. That said, follow these
tips, and you should do fine:
● Look for public parking
garages. Though more costly,
these are by far the most
convenient, as they are plen-
tiful (especially Downtown).
The garage under the
Common is the most eco-
nomical at $27 for 24 hours,
$6 for additional hours.
● Allow extra time. Some
destinations have garages
and/or valet, some don't.
If the latter, circle until you
get lucky enough to find an
empty spot on the street.
Look for side streets but be
careful not to park in "residents only" streets (which
include most).
● Pay attention to parking
signs on the street. Boston's
meter maids are merciless.

STUDENT TRAVELERS

● To get discounts on the T and admissions,
get an International Student Identity Card
(ISIC). If you are not a student but are under
26, get the International Youth Card (IYC).
● The Council on International Educational
Exchange (CIEE) has a Travel Service offering
domestic passes for bargain travel within the
US. It is also the exclusive agent for several
student-discount cards:
✉ 300 Fore Street, Portland, Maine
☎ 888/268-6245.
● Members of the Youth Hostel Association of
England and Wales (✉ Trevelyan House,
Dimple Road, Matlock, Derbyshire DE4 3YH
☎ 01629 592600) can use Hi-Boston hostels.
● Information on student hostels within the
US can be obtained from Hostelling
International–USA (✉ 8401 Colesville Road,
Suite 600, Silver Spring, MD 20910
☎ 301/495-1240; fax 301/495-6697;
email: admin_hienec@usahostels.org;
www.usahostels.org).

TELEPHONES

● The area code for Boston and Cambridge is
617. This must be included even when making
local calls. Some communities outside the city
have different area codes.
● To call the US from the UK dial 00 1,
followed by the area code and the number.
● To call the UK from the US, dial 011 44, then
drop the initial zero from the area code.

TICKETS

● The nine-day Boston CityPass (adult $44;
seniors and children ages 3–11 $28) gives free
admission for one visit each at five key sights:
the Museum of Fine Arts (▷ 70–71), the
Museum of Science (▷ 28–29), the New
England Aquarium (▷ 53), either the John F.
Kennedy Library and Museum (▷ 103) or
Harvard Museum of Natural History (▷ 91),
and Prudential Skywalk (▷ 73). Available
from the above sights or at the visitor

information center on Boston Common
(▷ 51), in the Prudential Center (▷ 73) or on
their website www.citypass.com/city/boston.

TOURIST OFFICES
● **Greater Boston Convention & Visitors
Bureau Inc.** ✉ 2 Copley Place, Suite 105,
Boston, MA 02116 ☎ 617/ 536-4100; fax
617/424-7664; www.bostonusa.com
● **Massachusetts Office of Travel & Tourism**
✉ State Transportation Building,
10 Park Plaza, Suite 4510, Boston, MA 02116
☎ 617/973-8500; fax 617/973-8525;
www.massvacation.com
● **Boston National Historical Park Visitor
Center** ✉ 15 State Street, opposite Old State
House ☎ 617/242-5642
● **Boston Common Information Kiosk**
✉ 148 Tremont Street ☎ 617/426-3115
● **Cambridge Office for Tourism**
✉ 4 Brattle Street, Harvard Square, Cambridge
☎ 617/441-2884

STAYING WIRED
Hopping on the internet is
increasingly easy in Boston;
many cafés in Back Bay (particularly on Newbury Street)
offer free wireless services,
as do many shops and salons
in the Back Bay area. The
Boston Public Library also
has free wireless internet
access and the entire downtown Salem has Wi-Fi.

EMERGENCY MEDICAL TREATMENT
Ambulance, fire, police	☎ 911
Massachusetts General Hospital	☎ 617/726-2000
Inn-House Doctor	☎ 617/859-1776 🕐 24 hours. Makes hotel visits
Late-night pharmacies: CVS	✉ Porter Square (35 White Street, near
	Massachusetts Avenue), Cambridge ☎ 617/876-5519
	🕐 24 hours
	✉ 587 Boylston Street, Back Bay ☎ 617/437-8414
	🕐 24 hours
Dental emergency	☎ 617/636-6828
Eye and Ear Infirmary	☎ 617/523-7900
Physician Referral Service	☎ 617/726-5800 🕐 Mon–Fri 8.30–4.45

CONSULATES
Canada	✉ 3 Copley Place ☎ 617/262-3760
Great Britain	✉ One Memorial Drive, Cambridge ☎ 617/245-4500
Ireland	✉ 535 Boylston Street ☎ 617/267-9330
Italy	✉ 600 Atlantic Avenue ☎ 617/722-9201
Portugal	✉ 899 Boylston Street ☎ 617/536-8740
Spain	✉ 31 St. James Avenue ☎ 617/536-2506

Timeline

REVOLUTION

In the 1760s Britain imposed taxes on her New England colonists. Increasingly angry at interference in their lucrative seafaring trade, the colonists, led by Sons of Freedom Sam Adams and John Hancock, protested at having to pay taxes when they had no representation in the government that was taxing them. Tension began to mount and on March 5, 1770 British soldiers killed five colonists in what became known as the Boston Massacre. On December 16, 1773, Patriots protested against the Tea Act by throwing tea into the sea (the Boston Tea Party). British retaliation made war inevitable.

From left: American Revolution re-enactment; statue of a Minute Man on the spot where events sparked the revolution; plaque on the grave of Samuel Adams; equestrian statue of Paul Revere; obelisk commemorating the Battle of Bunker Hill

Pre-1620 The Algonquins inhabit the Boston area.

1620 Pilgrims arrive on the *Mayflower* and establish the first English colony in Plymouth.

1629 Puritans found the Massachusetts Bay Colony in Charlestown.

1630 The colony moves to Beacon Hill on the Shawmut Peninsula.

1636 Harvard College is founded.

1680 Most of Boston is concentrated in what is to become the North End, around the flourishing seaport.

1775 The Revolution starts in Boston.

1776 The British leave Boston on March 17. On July 18, the Declaration of Independence is read from the State House balcony.

1790s Trade with China brings prosperity.

1795 Architect Charles Bulfinch starts the new State House. Five years later he helps to develop Beacon Hill.

1826 Mayor Josiah Quincy extends the waterfront and builds Quincy Market.

1840s Irish immigrants, fleeing the Potato Famine, pour into the North End.

1856 Work begins on filling in and developing the Back Bay as a new residential area.

1877 Swan Boats—distinctive boats with large model swans at the helm—come to the Public Garden.

1897 The Boston marathon is launched.

1918 The Red Sox win baseball's World Series—their first pennant victory. Their next victory was not to be until 2004.

1960s–70s An extensive urban renewal scheme includes John Hancock Tower.

1990 The US's biggest art theft occurs at the Isabella Stewart Gardner Museum.

1995 FleetCenter replaces the Boston Garden, home of the Bruins (ice hockey) and Celtics (basketball).

2004 New England Patriots win the Super Bowl for the second time since 2002. The Boston Red Sox win the World Series championship for the first time in almost a century.

2006 The Big Dig, Boston's decade-long, large-scale construction project to ease Boston's huge traffic problem, finally ends.

2009 Senator Edward Kennedy, the political face of Massachusetts on the national and international scene for over 40 years, dies.

PAUL REVERE'S RIDE

In his lifetime Paul Revere (1735–1818) was known as a silversmith, but he was immortalized—with some poetic license—as a hero of the Revolution by the poet Henry Wadsworth Longfellow. Revere was a messenger for the Sons of Liberty and on the eve of the first battle of the Revolution rode to Lexington to warn local militia men about British preparations.

JFK

John Fitzgerald Kennedy was born in the Boston suburb of Brookline in 1917. His grandfather, "Honey-Fitz," was one of a long line of Irish mayors. Kennedy was elected president in 1960—good-looking and charismatic, he was a symbol of the nation's hope for a progressive future. He was assassinated on November 22, 1963.

NEED TO KNOW TIMELINE

Index

A

accommodations 107–112
  bed-and-breakfast 109, 111
  hotels 109–112
Adams Gallery 54
African Meeting House 25, 38
airports 116–117
alcohol 82, 119, 120
Ames Building 38
Arlington Street Church 54
Arnold Arboretum 17, 104
art and antiques 10, 12, 41, 42, 72, 94
art deco buildings 54
Arthur M. Sackler Museum 91

B

Back Bay 67
Back Bay and the South End 63–84
  entertainment and nightlife 82–83
  map 64–65
  restaurants 84
  shopping 72, 80–81
  sights 66–78
  walk 79
ballet and modern dance 18, 60, 96
banks 120
baseball 5, 78
Beacon Hill 8, 24–25
Beacon Hill to Charlestown 20–46
  entertainment and nightlife 43
  map 22–23
  restaurants 45–46
  shopping 41–42
  sights 24–39
  walk 40
bed-and-breakfast 109, 111
bicycle paths 118
Black Heritage Trail 39
book stores 10, 12, 58, 94, 95
Boston Athenaeum 8, 50
Boston Common 8, 51
Boston Common to the Waterfront 47–62
  entertainment and nightlife 59–60
  map 48–49
  restaurants 61–62
  shopping 58
  sights 50–56
  walk 57
Boston environs 99–106
  excursions 105–106
  map 100–101

sights 102–104
Boston Fire Museum 54
Boston Harbor Islands 9, 102
Boston Public Library 9, 66, 82
Boston Women's Memorial 17, 67
Brattle Street 92
budget travelers 18, 109
Bulfinch, Charles 24, 27, 35, 39
Bumpkin Island 102
Bunker Hill Monument 37
Busch-Reisinger Museum 91
buses 117, 118

C

Cambridge 85–98
  entertainment and nightlife 96–97
  map 86–87
  restaurants 97–98
  shopping 94–95
  sights 88–92
  walk 93
car rental 116, 119
Charles River 38, 78
Charles Street 41, 42
Charlestown 36–37
Cheers 43
children 12, 18
Children's Museum 18, 54
Chinatown 13, 14, 55, 57, 62
Christopher Columbus Waterfront Park 38
cinema 83, 96
climate and seasons 114
clubs and bars 13
  see also entertainment and nightlife
comedy clubs 43, 59, 60
Commonwealth Avenue 9, 67
Concord 106
consulates 123
Copp's Hill Burying Ground 31
crafts 11, 12, 42, 80, 94
credit cards 120, 122
Custom House Tower 17, 38

D

dental treatment 123
department stores 12, 80, 81
disabilities, visitors with 118
driving 117, 119, 122

E

eating out 14
  see also restaurants
Emerald Necklace 4, 67, 78
entertainment and nightlife 13

Back Bay and the South End 82–83
  Beacon Hill to Charlestown 43
  Boston Common to the Waterfront 59–60
  Cambridge 96–97
Esplanade 16, 38, 78
events and festivals 114
excursions 105–106

F

Faneuil Hall and Marketplace 9, 26, 41
fashion shopping 10, 11, 12, 16, 41, 42, 58, 72, 80, 81, 95, 96
Federal Reserve Bank of Boston 55
Fens 17, 78
Fenway Park 78
Filene's Basement 80
First Church of Christ, Scientist 78
Fogg Art Museum 91
food and drink
  alcohol 82, 119, 120
  baked beans 10, 46
  New England dishes 46
  seafood 18, 45, 46, 61, 62, 98
  shopping for 12, 41, 42, 94, 95
  vegetarian food 15, 62
  see also eating out; restaurants
Fort Warren 102
Franklin Park Zoo 104
Frederick Law Olmsted National Historic Site 104

G

Georges Island 102
gifts and souvenirs 10, 12
Gillette Stadium 104
Grape Island 102

H

Harrison Gray Otis House 9, 27
Harvard Museum of Natural History (HMNH) 91
Harvard Square 9, 89, 93, 94–95
Harvard University 4, 9, 88–89
Harvard University museums 9, 90–91
history 124–125
Hobbamock's Homesite 105
hostels 122
hotels 109–112

I

Institute of Contemporary Art (ICA) 52
insurance 120

internet access 123
internet café 115
Irish Famine Memorial 55
Isabella Stewart Gardner
    Museum 9, 16, 68–69

J
James Curley statue 38
JFK Library and Museum 9, 103
JFK National Historic Site 104
John Hancock Tower 17, 77

K
Kennedy, J. F. 103, 104, 125
King's Chapel and Burying
    Ground 55

L
Larz Anderson Auto Museum 104
Lexington 106
licensing laws 82, 120
Longfellow House 92
lost property 122
Louisburg Square 24
Lovells Island 102

M
Mapparium 78
maps
    Back Bay and the South End
        64–65
    Beacon Hill to Charlestown
        22–23
    Boston Common to the
        Waterfront 48–49
    Boston environs 100–101
    Cambridge 86–87
Mayflower II 105
medical treatment 123
MIT buildings 92
MIT sculptures 92
money 120
Mount Auburn Cemetery 92
Museum of Afro-American
    History 38
Museum of Fine Arts 9, 18,
    70–71, 83
museum opening hours 121
museum pass 122–123
Museum of Science 9, 18, 28–29
music venues 43, 59, 60, 82, 83,
    96, 97

N
New England Aquarium 9, 16,
    18, 53
New England Holocaust
    Memorial 39

Newbury Street 8, 10, 11, 72,
    80, 81
newspapers and magazines 120
Nichols House Museum 25, 39
North End 8, 13, 30–31, 34

O
Old Granary Burying Ground
    40, 55
Old North Church 8, 31
Old South Meeting House 56
Old State House 8, 32–33
opening hours 120–121
outdoor gear and clothing 12,
    42, 58, 80, 81

P
Park Street Church 56
parking 119, 122
passports and visas 116
Paul Revere House 8, 34
Paul Revere Mall 31
Paul Revere statue 39
Peabody Museum 91
Peabody Essex Museum 106
Peddocks Island 102
pedicabs 119
pharmacies 123
Pilgrim Hall Museum 105
Plimoth Plantation 105
Plymouth 105
Plymouth National Wax
    Museum 105
Plymouth Rock 105
Post Office Square 56
Prudential Center 8, 73, 81
Prudential Tower 17, 73
Public Garden 6, 16, 17, 51
public holidays 121
public transportation 115,
    118–119

Q
Quincy Market, see Faneuil
    Marketplace

R
restaurants 13, 14, 15
    Back Bay and the South End 84
    Beacon Hill to Charlestown
        45–46
    Boston Common to the
        Waterfront 61–62
    Cambridge 97–98
Revere, Paul 34, 35, 39, 55,
    106, 125
river tours 38, 43
Robert Gould Shaw Memorial
    17, 56

S
safety, personal 121
Salem 106
Samuel Adams statue 39
Sears Building 38
shopping 10–12, 16
    Back Bay and the South End
        72, 80–81
    Beacon Hill to Charlestown
        41–42
    Boston Common to the
        Waterfront 58
    Cambridge 94–95
skyscrapers 17, 54
Skywalk 8, 13, 73
Sleepy Hollow Cemetery 106
smoking etiquette 121
South End 8, 74–75
SoWa district 75
State House 8, 35
student travelers 122
subway system 118

T
taxis 119
TD Garden 39
telephones 122
theater 18, 43, 59, 60, 82, 83, 96,
    97
ticket outlets 59
time differences 114
tourist information 115, 123
train services 117, 119
traveler's checks 120, 121, 122
Trinity Church 8, 16, 76–77

U
USS Constitution 8, 36–37

V
views over the city 17, 38, 73
visitor passes 118, 122–123

W
walks
    Beacon Hill 40
    Boston Common to the
        Waterfront 57
    Harvard Square 93
    South End 79
websites 115
whale-watching 16, 53

Z
zoo 104

Boston's
25 BEST

WRITTEN BY Sue Gordon
ADDITIONAL WRITING Alexandra Hall and Michael Blanding
UPDATED BY Paul Franklin and Nancy Mikula
DESIGN WORK Jacqueline Bailey
COVER DESIGN Tigist Getachew
INDEXER Marie Lorimer
IMAGE RETOUCHING AND REPRO Sarah Montgomery and James Tims
REVIEWING EDITOR Linda Schmidt
PROJECT EDITOR Marie-Claire Jefferies
SERIES EDITOR Marie-Claire Jefferies

ISBN 978-1-4000-0540-6

SEVENTH EDITION

IMPORTANT TIP
Time inevitably brings changes, so always confirm prices, travel facts, and other perishable information when it matters. Although Fodor's cannot accept responsibility for errors, you can use this guide in the confidence that we have taken every care to ensure its accuracy.

SPECIAL SALES
This book is available for special discounts for bulk purchases for sales promotions or premiums. Special editions, including personalized covers, excerpts of existing books, and corporate imprints, can be created in large quantities for special needs. For more information, write to Special Markets/Premium Sales, 1745 Broadway, MD 6–2, New York, NY 10019 or email specialmarkets@randomhouse.com.

Color separation by AA Digital Department
Printed and bound by Leo Paper Products, China
10 9 8 7 6 5 4 3 2 1

A04202
Maps in this title produced from mapping © MAIRDUMONT / Falk Verlag 2011
Transport map © Communicarta Ltd, UK

The Automobile Association wishes to thank the following photographers, companies and picture libraries for their assistance in the preparation of this book.

Abbreviations for the picture credits are as follows – (t) top; (b) bottom; (l) left; (r) right; (c) centre; (AA) AA World Travel Library.

1 AA/J Nicholson; 2 AA/M Lynch; 3 AA/M Lynch; 4t AA/M Lynch; 4c AA/M Lynch; 5t AA/M Lynch; 5c AA/C Sawyer; 6t AA/M Lynch; 6cl AA/C Sawyer; 6c AA/M Lynch; 6cr AA/M Lynch; 6bl AA/C Sawyer; 6bcl AA/C Sawyer; 6bcr AA/C Coe; 6br Photodisc; 7t AA/M Lynch; 7cl AA/J Nicholson; 7cr AA/C Sawyer; 7bl AA/M Lynch; 7bc AA/J Nicholson; 7br AA/M Lynch; 8 AA/M Lynch; 9 AA/M Lynch; 10t AA/M Lynch; 10ct AA/C Sawyer; 10c AA/C Sawyer; 10/11cb AA/D Clapp; 10/11b AA/C Coe; 11t AA/M Lynch; 11ct AA/M Lynch; 11c AA/C Sawyer; 12 AA/M Lynch; 13t AA/M Lynch; 13tct AA/C Sawyer; 13ct AA/J Nicholson; 13c AA/D Clapp; 13cb Brand X Pictures; 13b AA/M Lynch; 14t AA/M Lynch; 14ct AA/C Sawyer; 14c AA/C Sawyer; 14cb AA/C Sawyer; 14b AA/C Sawyer; 15t AA/M Lynch; 15b AA/D Clapp; 16t AA/M Lynch; 16ct AA/M Lynch; 16c AA/C Sawyer; 16cb AA/C Sawyer; 16b AA/J Nicholson; 17t AA/M Lynch; 17ct AA/C Sawyer; 17c AA/M Lynch; 17cb AA/C Sawyer; 17b AA/C Sawyer; 18t AA/M Lynch; 18ct AA/C Sawyer; 18c AA/J Nicholson; 18cb AA/C Sawyer; 18b AA/P Kenward; 19t AA/J Nicholson; 19ct AA/C Sawyer; 19c AA/J Nicholson; 19cb AA/C Coe; 19b AA/C Sawyer; 20/21 AA/D Clapp; 24tl AA/C Sawyer; 24cl AA/C Sawyer; 24cr AA/C Sawyer; 24/25t AA/C Coe; 24/25c AA/C Coe; 25r AA/J Nicholson; 26l AA/C Sawyer; 26r AA/J Nicholson; 27l AA/C Sawyer; 27r AA/C Sawyer; 28l AA/C Sawyer; 28/9t AA/C Sawyer; 28/9b AA/C Sawyer; 29tr Museum of Science, Boston; 29bl AA/D Clapp; 29br AA/D Clapp; 30 AA/C Sawyer; 30/1 AA/C Sawyer; 31 AA/M Lynch; 32 AA/J Nicholson; 32/3 AA/C Sawyer; 34l AA/J Nicholson; 34c AA/C Sawyer; 34r AA/C Coe; 35l AA/J Nicholson; 35r AA/C Coe; 36 AA/C Coe; 36/37t AA/C Sawyer; 36/37b AA/J Nicholson; 37l AA/C Coe; 37r AA/J Nicholson; 38t AA/C Sawyer; 38bl Greater Boston Convention & Visitors Bureau; 38br A/C Sawyer; 39t AA/C Sawyer; 39bl AA/J Nicholson; 39br Museum of African American History; 40 AA/J Nicholson; 41 AA/D Clapp; 42 AA/C Sawyer; 43 Digital Vision; 44 Photodisc; 45 AA/C Sawyer; 46 AA/C Sawyer; 47 AA/D Clapp; 50l © Image Management/Alamy; 50r © Visual Mining/Alamy 51 AA/M Lynch; 52l The Institute of Contemporary Art/Boston, Diller Scofidio + Renfro Architects, Photo: (c) Iwan Baan; 52r Founders' Gallery, The Institute of Contemporary Art/Boston, Diller Scofidio + Renfro Architects, Photo: Peter Vanderwarker; 53l AA/C Sawyer; 53r AA/C Sawyer; 54t AA/C Sawyer; 54b AA/C Sawyer; 55t AA/C Sawyer; 55b AA/C Sawyer; 56t AA/C Sawyer; 56bl Old South Meeting House; 56br AA/C Sawyer; 57 AA/J Nicholson; 58 AA/S McBride; 59 Digital Vision; 60 Brand X Pictures; 61 AA/P Bennett; 62 Bananastock; 63 AA/C Coe; 66l AA/C Sawyer; 66r AA/C Sawyer; 67l AA/C Sawyer; 67r AA/C Coe; 68/69 Courtesy of the Isabella Stewart Gardner Museum, Boston; 69 Courtesy of the Isabella Stewart Gardner Museum, Boston; 70 Photo © Tony Rinaldo images, photo courtesy of the Museum of Fine Arts, Boston; 70/71 AA/C Sawyer; 72l AA/C Sawyer; 72r AA/C Sawyer; 73l AA/J Nicholson; 73c AA/C Sawyer; 73r AA/D Clapp; 74 AA/J Nicholson; 74/75 AA/J Nicholson; 76 AA/M Lynch; 76/77 AA/C Sawyer; 77 AA/C Sawyer; 78t AA/C Sawyer; 78b AA/M Lynch; 79 AA/J Nicholson; 80 AA/C Sawyer; 81 AA/C Sawyer; 82 Photodisc; 83 Digital Vision; 84 Brand X Pictures; 85 AA/C Coe; 88l AA/M Lynch; 88/9t AA/M Lynch; 88/9b AA/M Lynch; 89t AA/C Coe; 89bl AA/C Sawyer; 89br AA/M Lynch; 90 AA/C Sawyer; 91l AA/C Sawyer; 91r AA/C Sawyer; 92t AA/C Sawyer; 92bl AA/M Lynch; 92br AA/J Nicholson; 93 AA/J Nicholson; 94 AA/J A Tims; 95 AA/C Sawyer; 96 Brand X Pictures; 97t Photodisc; 97c AA/D Corrance; 98 AA/T Souter; 99 AA/M Lynch; 102 Photolibrary; 103l Kennedy Presidential Library; 103r Kennedy Presidential Library; 104t AA/C Sawyer; 104b AA/C Sawyer; 105 AA/P Bennett; 106t AA/P Bennett; 106bl AA/J Lynch; 106bcl AA/C Coe; 106bc AA/C Coe; 106bcr AA/C Sawyer; 106br AA/J Lynch; 107 AA/C Sawyer; 108t AA/C Sawyer; 108ct AA/M Lynch; 108c AA/C Sawyer; 108cb AA/S McBride; 108b AA/C Sawyer; 109 AA/C Sawyer; 110 AA/C Sawyer; 111 AA/C Sawyer; 112 AA/C Sawyer; 113 AA/C Sawyer; 114 AA/C Coe; 115 AA/C Coe; 116 AA/C Coe; 117 AA/C Coe; 118 AA/C Coe; 119 AA/C Coe; 120t AA/C Coe; 120b MRI Bankers' Guide to Foreign Currency; 121t AA/C Coe; 121b AA/M Lynch; 122 AA/C Coe; 123 AA/C Coe; 124t AA/C Coe; 124bl AA/J Lynch; 124br AA/C Sawyer; 125t AA/C Coe; 125bl AA/C Coe; 125bc AA/C Sawyer; 125br AA/C Sawyer.

Every effort has been made to trace the copyright holders, and we apologise in advance for any unintentional omissions or errors. We would be pleased to apply any corrections in any following edition of this publication.